The Paths of Soaring Flight

The Paths of Soaring Flight

Frank Irving

Formerly of Dept. of Aeronautics, Imperial College

Imperial College Press

ICP

Published by

Imperial College Press
203 Electrical Engineering Building
Imperial College
London SW7 2BT

Distributed by

World Scientific Publishing Co. Pte. Ltd.
P O Box 128, Farrer Road, Singapore 912805
USA office: Suite 1B, 1060 Main Street, River Edge, NJ 07661
UK office: 57 Shelton Street, Covent Garden, London WC2H 9HE

British Library Cataloguing-in-Publication Data
A catalogue record for this book is available from the British Library.

ISBN   1-86094-055-2

Printed in Singapore.

For Ann Welch and in memory of the late Lorne Welch

Sincere thanks are due to Jane Lewis
for her invaluable assistance in helping the
author with the obscurities of the computer.

The cover photograph is by Neil Stuart Lawson,
and shows Afandi Darlington flying 96, the ASW-24
belonging to Imperial College Gliding Club.

Other publication by F. G. Irving, MEng, DIC, CEng, FRAeS:

An Introduction to the Longitudinal Static Stability of Low-Speed Aircraft,
Pergamon, 1966.

With A. and L. Welch: *The Soaring Pilot*, John Murray, 1955, 1957.
                     The New Soaring Pilot, 1968, 1970, 1977.

(Also published in USA as *The Complete Soaring Pilot's Handbook*, David
McKay Company Inc., New York.)

...and numerous contributions to OSTIV, some of which are mentioned
in the present work. (See Apendix I.)

FOREWORD

This is being written 107 years after Otto Lilienthal made his maiden flight in his first hang-glider, 103 years since Percy Pilcher flew, and 95 years after the Wright brothers took to the air in their rather more conventional machine at Kill Devil Hill. So we are celebrating about a century of successful human flight, throughout which unpowered aerodynes, from Lilienthal's hang glider to modern sailplanes (and not forgetting the Space Shuttle) have introduced major innovations to aeronautics. The first machines provided the very foundations of flight; the Vampyr (1921) used the first leading edge torsion-box structure; in the late 1920s — an era in which most powered aeroplanes showed a cheerful disregard of profile drag — sailplanes began to look rather as they do today; in the 1930s, wings became thinner to deal with the demands of cross-country flying, and the whole machine became stronger in the pursuit of cloud flying; in the 1950s, extensive natural laminar boundary layers were being pursued; in the 1960s, the first all-composite flying machine with an aerofoil designed specifically for sailplanes, flew in the World Gliding Championships. Since then, we have seen the use of more exotic plastics and continuing advances in the techniques of low-loss aerodynamics.

Once it became apparent that the atmosphere was a source of energy capable of sustaining flying machines, the contributions of soaring to meteorology have been equally significant. Much of the knowledge of the structure of atmospheric turbulence was made by pilots using thermals, from 1929 onwards. Similarly, lee waves were the subject of intensive investigations, particularly in the 1950s, leading to comprehensive mathematical theories.

Nearly all of this effort has been in the pursuit of the sport of soaring, an occupation whose many facets include its intellectual fascination. It has been noted that all of the materials required to construct a good sailplane were available hundreds of years ago, and at least one work of fiction ("The Woolacombe Bird" by Ann Welch, Jonathon Cape, 1964) has been based on this observation. But it needed the sort of thinking which went with the blossoming of technology in the 19th and 20th centuries, and the corresponding increase in leisure time, to make it really happen. It is a happy coincidence (or perhaps a manifestation of the Anthropic principle) that the properties of materials, the motions of the atmosphere and the mass of individual people, all conspire to make it possible.

In such circumstances, both the machines and the techniques of using them require the generous application of technology. From the point of view of the soaring pilot, he can make quite a lot of headway on the basis of physical explanation but, ultimately, a certain amount of numeracy is required. For example, the physical basis of the British handicapping system seems straightforward enough, but carrying out the calculations for a new type of sailplane is not a negligible exercise.

So this book is aimed at the Numerate Pilot, who wants to know the basis of the design parameters of his machine, how it performs in various circumstances, the various ideas relating to optimising its overall performance and their practicability. This is not a "how to do it" book: there are plenty of those, some written by better pilots than myself. Nor is it intended to present lengthy passages of profound mathematics: it does present some of the really fundamental concepts in detail, but mostly it displays results so that the Enquiring Numerate Soaring Pilot can dig deeper, if so inclined. Some readers may be surprised to find that there exists such a quantity of endeavour, often quite profound, and all devoted to the furthering of a sport. Moreover, what appears here is little more than the tip of an iceberg: there is an enormous background of airworthiness, structural and aerodynamic design, stability and control, meteorology and electronics and indeed, much of the stock in trade of professional aeronautics. We should be happy that so many people exercise their talents in the pursuit of better soaring.

Much of this book is concerned with matters which are fundamental to the understanding of soaring, such as energy heights and inter-thermal speeds. It may come as a surprise that some of these concepts are markedly more subtle than first acquaintance would suggest. There are also some bits of analysis which depend on the pilot having powers of prophecy. Where is the next thermal? How strong is it? How does its strength vary with height? What is the point of such considerations, you may ask, when the pilot's powers of prophecy are so limited? Maybe this book will provide some answers.

In writing this book, it seemed important to gather together many of the fundamental ideas which have made modern soaring possible before they are lost, because some of them lurk in obscure or out-of-print documents. The choice is mine, but I hope that readers will find it suitable.

F G Irving
Lasham, 1998

CONTENTS

for motor sailplanes. Performance in turning flight. Best gliding angle and minimum sink. Effect of ballast and flaps. Performance in turning flight. Ground effect.

The measurement of vertical velocity. The concept of Total Energy. Methods of compensating variometers: venturis, the Irving tube. Air mass-movement indicators. Electric variometers.

Other instruments. The altimeter and its calibration. The airspeed indicator: pitot and static sources, pressure errors and their effect on limitations and best speeds to fly; calibration; other errors. Reduction of never-exceed speed with height to avoid flutter.

Thermals: observations in the laboratory and in the atmosphere. Mathematical descriptions: power laws: spherical bubbles: general remarks. Cloud streets. Waves. The wind. The Standard Atmosphere.

Flying in thermals. A little history. The classical analysis. Best speeds to fly and the effect of down-draughts. Average speed attained. The BGA handicapping system.

The practice of cross-country flying. The MacCready ring and its calibration. Tricks with variometers. Practical considerations and techniques. Use of flaps.

SECTION A:
THE SAILPLANE IN STILL AIR

Chapter 1

UNITS, AND SOME BASIC IDEAS

Units

On the assumption that the main readership of this book is likely to speak English as a native language, the units are mainly those approved by ICAO for non-metric countries. At present, however, some confusion exists in the UK. The reader would undoubtedly have been educated metrically and is probably accustomed to speeds in m/s and forces in newtons, and then he enters the world of practical aviation and finds speeds in knots and forces in pounds (strictly, pounds-force). Moreover, since most sailplanes originate in Germany, we are accustomed to masses in kilograms and the location of the centre of gravity in millimetres from some datum. Here, we will generally settle for speeds, both along the flight path and in the vertical direction in knots, masses in pounds, forces in pounds-force and heights in feet. This instantly introduces some bother, for if air density were in lb/ft^3, then aerodynamic forces would be in poundals. To cause forces to be in pounds-force, we invent a unit for air density called the *slug*, so that air densities are in $slugs/ft^3$. A slug is thus 31.740 lb. (There is a corresponding quantity in metric units.) Whilst mainly using English units, we will occasionally use the metric system, whichever may be convenient. A list of relevant conversion factors is given in Appendix II.

Dimensionless Coefficients and Other Numbers

Aeronautical engineers are notoriously fond of dimensionless quantities, and very convenient they are when you are accustomed to them. We will try to keep the use of such quantities to a minimum but a few are inescapable, particularly the coefficients used to describe the characteristics of wing sections. Thus, the lift coefficient is:

$$C_L = L \Big/ \tfrac{1}{2}\rho V^2 S . \tag{1.1}$$

(See the Table of Symbols for the meanings of the various symbols.)

The effect of this is that the smaller V is, the greater will be the lift coefficient and vice-versa. Also, the magnitude of the lift coefficient will be independent of the system of units in use. In nearly level flight, $L = W$, approximately, and under these conditions, a lift coefficient of about 0.13 would correspond to the never-exceed speed of the average sailplane, and 1.5–1.6 would be about the maximum value for an unflapped wing.

The "$\tfrac{1}{2}$" which appears in this equation is not essential to make the the coefficient dimensionless and indeed, for quite a long time, it was omitted. However, it is convenient to include it because $\tfrac{1}{2}\rho V^2$ is the dynamic head of Bernoulli's equation.

In an exactly similar fashion, we can define a drag coefficient:

$$C_D = D \Big/ \tfrac{1}{2}\rho V^2 S \tag{1.2}$$

and 0.005–0.006 would be about the minimum drag coefficient of a two-dimensional wing section at sailplane Reynolds numbers.

Both the lift and drag coefficients will be functions of other dimensionless quantities, in this case the angle of attack or incidence and the Reynolds number. The Reynolds number expresses the ratio of the inertial forces in a fluid to the viscous forces and has the value $\rho V l / \mu$. Here, l is a reference length, such as the chord of a wing. (See, for example, Anderson, 1991.) For sailplane wings, R_e would normally lie between 0.5×10^6 and 5.0×10^6. This is a pretty unfortunate range to be in, since the characteristics of wing sections are changing fairly rapidly with Reynolds number. Strictly, these coefficients are also functions of

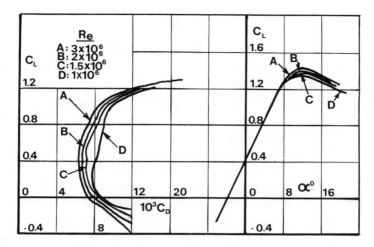

Fig. 1.1. The characteristics of a two-dimensional aerofoil. The curves on the left are presented as "polars" (i.e., the angle of incidence has been eliminated), whilst the curves on the right are simply lift coefficient against incidence.

Mach number, V/a, but this quantity is unlikely to be significant at the speeds of sailplanes.

The characteristics of a two-dimensional wing could therefore be presented as a series of curves of C_L and C_D vs. angle of incidence, α, for various values of R_e. (See Fig. 1.1.) Also, it is possible to omit the angle of incidence, and to present the characteristics of an aerofoil as a series of curves of C_D against C_L at various Reynolds numbers. This was due to a suggestion by Otto Lilienthal, who called the result the "polar diagram". (See Prandtl and Tietjens, 1934, p. 147.) Later, this expression was applied to the curve of rate of sink as a function of forward speed for a complete sailplane.

Lift Curve Slope

The above curves of C_L vs. α are quite close to straight lines at angles of incidence below the stall and it may be shown that, in incompressible flow, with viscosity neglected but with the Kutta-Joukowski condition satisfied, the lift coefficient of a thin two-dimensional wing will be:

$$C_L = 2\pi\alpha .$$ (1.3)

The lift curve slope is therefore 2π for α in radians, or about 0.11 for α in degrees. Practical values are remarkably close to this value (Kuethe and Chow, 1986, p. 122), but may be slightly more or less. We shall see later that a finite aspect ratio reduces the value somewhat.

True and Equivalent Speeds

It will have been noted that the dynamic head is $\frac{1}{2}\rho V^2$, where ρ is the local air density and V the true airspeed. This can equally be written $\frac{1}{2}\rho_o V_i^2$, where ρ_o is the standard sea-level air density and V_i is known as the equivalent airspeed. Hence $V_i = V(\rho/\rho_o)^{\frac{1}{2}}$. Equally, the dynamic head which appears in the expressions for the lift and drag can be expressed in either fashion. Writing the lift as $C_L \frac{1}{2}\rho_o V_i^2 S$, we see that the number of independent variables has been reduced by one. Also, for a given glider at a given weight, with a fixed value of $C_{L\max}$, the stalling speed will occur at a fixed value of the equivalent airspeed. This is particularly useful because, as shown in Chapter 6, the reading of the airspeed indicator is approximately the equivalent airspeed, or at any rate, if the EAS is fixed, so is the IAS. This is also true for most other significant speeds: for example, the speed for best gliding angle of the above sailplane will also occur at a fixed EAS.

Boundary Layers

The most important aspect of the flow about an aerofoil to be affected by Reynolds number is the flow in the boundary layer. This is the thin layer of air adjacent to the surface of a wing or any other body in the airstream, where the local velocity is reduced by skin friction, becoming zero at the surface. There is a tendency to think of boundary layers as being of almost imperceptible thickness under normal circumstances, but not so. Towards the trailing edge of a low-drag wing at a typical sailplane Reynolds number, it could well be a couple of centimetres thick on the upper surface. In 1883, Osborne Reynolds showed that there are two types of flow in the boundary layer: laminar, where the paths of particles are substantially parallel to the surface, and turbulent, where the motion of the particles is altogether less organised and, in particular, high-speed particles from the outer parts of the layer can move down towards the surface. (See Simons, 1978, for a good account of boundary layers. This is in the context of models, but it is well worth reading.)

The behaviour of the boundary layer, and hence the skin friction which it produces, depends on the pressure gradients to which it has been subjected, the Reynolds number (i.e., the instantaneous value, based on the distance between the start of the boundary layer to the point under consideration) and imperfections in the surface.

These remarks relate mainly to two-dimensional boundary layers, and matters become markedly more complicated in three dimensions. Modern sailplanes are substantially free from surface defects, save for the discontinuities at control surfaces. A boundary layer will start life in the laminar condition at the leading edge and, at the Reynolds numbers of sailplanes, will remain so, until somewhere around the minimum pressure point on that surface. Now a laminar boundary layer produces markedly less drag than a turbulent one, so it would seem desirable to get the minimum pressure point on, say the top surface of a wing, as far aft as possible. But this produces other problems: for example, the increasing pressure gradient behind it may become high enough to lead to premature separation of the turbulent layer. The point at which a laminar layer becomes turbulent is known as the *transition point*, although it is actually a region of finite width (see Fig. 1.2), and it is accompanied by a thickening of the layer in order that momentum may be preserved. Either a laminar or a turbulent layer may separate from the surface over which it is flowing, when the velocity close to the surface has diminished to such an extent that the vertical velocity gradient has become zero. Broadly speaking, laminar separation which is not followed by re-attachment will be unusual on sailplanes. But transition often occurs by the laminar layer separating, becoming turbulent and re-attaching. One effect of this process is that the drag which results is markedly higher than if transition had occurred without the laminar separation bubble, as it is known. Various attempts are made to suppress the laminar separation, thus obtaining a normal transition. This is done either by a

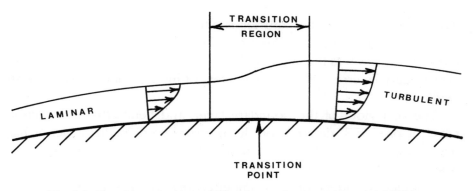

Fig. 1.2. Transition on an aerofoil without a laminar separation bubble.

gentle flow of air from a pitot tube through small holes just ahead of the separation bubble, or by zig-zag tape, but such methods only work if the minimum pressure point is in a fixed position over a wide array of circumstances (Althaus, 1991). On the lower surface of a wing, it is possible to fix such a point at about 80% chord; placing the zig-zag tape at 77% chord to supress the laminar bubble will then lead to a significant drag reduction (Boermans and Waibel, 1989). It is not possible to apply this technique to the upper surface of a wing because the minimum pressure point is much more mobile. In general, the use of tape is only feasible on wing sections specifically designed to take it, although its use may be beneficial just ahead of control surfaces.

Designing a wing section with a low minimum drag coefficient, a good spread of low drag vs. lift coefficient, and a high $C_{L\max}$, requires pushing boundary layer theory to about its current limit, but it would be folly to suppose that the absolute limit has been achieved. Figure 1.3 shows the characteristics of a modern section.

It is usual to assume that the best surface is totally smooth, but some work at NASA has shown that the skin friction under the turbulent boundary layer can be reduced if the surface has streamwise grooves or "riblets" (Kuethe and Chow, 1986). The riblets are pretty fine, roughly comparable with the surface of an LP record. The snags are that they must be quite accurately aligned with the local flow direction and, in a laminar region, they will trigger transition to turbulent flow.

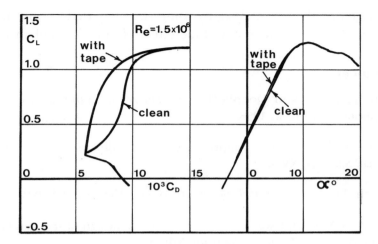

Fig. 1.3. The characteristics of a modern two-dimensional aerofoil section. The section is DU-84-158 at a Reynolds number of 1.5 million. The tape is of the zig-zag type, with a chordwise dimension of 11 mm and a width, perpendicular to one limb of the tape, of 3 mm. The thickness is 0.5 mm. The decrease in drag with the tape fitted is most marked.

The Effect of Flaps

Figure 1.3 shows the properties of an unflapped section of reasonable thickness, about 16%. Increasing the thickness will broaden the C_L – range (i.e., the range of lift coefficient over which the drag coefficient is reasonably low. In the days of NACA 6-series wings, this was very well defined, but nowadays it is comparatively vague. Hence the "reasonable" in the above sentence.) But the actual value of the minimum drag coefficient is increased and, broadly speaking, the two effects will largely cancel out. The application of a small flap at the trailing edge enables us to escape from this quandary: by changing the flap setting, the camber is effectively altered. A small downward deflection will move the minimum drag coefficient in the direction of higher lift coefficients, but leaves its value much the same. At the same time, the angle of zero lift becomes more negative, and hence the changes in the incidence of the fuselage are somewhat reduced, compared with those of an un-flapped sailplane. So, we can get the lower drag of a thin wing and the

C_L – range of a thick one. Also, by using large flap deflections, the landing speed can be decreased and the effect of airbrakes enhanced.

References

Abbott, I.A. and von Doenhoff, A.E, *Theory of Wing Sections*, Dover Publications, New York, 1958.

Althaus, D., "Performance Improvements on Tailplanes by Turbulators", *Technical Soaring*, XV, **4**.

Anderson, J.D., *Fundamentals of Aerodynamics*, McGraw-Hill, 1991.

Boermans, L.M.M. and Waibel, G., "Aerodynamic design of the standard class sailplane ASW-24", *Technical Soaring*, XIII, **3**.

Kuethe, A.M. and Chow, C-Y., *Foundations of Aerodynamics*, John Wiley and Sons, 1986.

Prandtl, L. and Teitjens O.G., *Applied Hydro- and Aeromechanics*, Dover Publications, New York, 1934 and 1957.

Simons, M., *Model Aircraft Aerodynamics*, Model and Allied Publications, Herts., 1978.

Chapter 2

WINGS AND WINGLETS

Wings of Finite Span

The previous chapter dealt with two-dimensional wings (i.e., wings of infinite aspect ratio). But any real wing has a finite span and therefore produces an "induced" drag, basically due to imparting downwards momentum to some of the air through which it is passing, in order to produce the lift (Prandtl and Teitjens, 1934, pp. 185–225). Another way of looking at this situation is to note that on a lifting wing, the average pressure on the lower surface exceeds atmospheric, whilst on the upper surface it is less than atmospheric. Towards the wingtips, this pressure difference tends to disappear, leading to an outwards drift of the air below the wing and an inwards flow on top. At the wingtip, the opposing velocities will cause the air leaving the wing to form a vortex. In fact, the above inward and outward velocities will cause vortices to be shed all the way across the span and, for a given span, the induced drag will depend on the spanwise distribution of the trailing vorticity which, in turn, will depend on the spanwise distribution of lift.

There is another way of envisaging this situation. Over the upper surface of a lifting wing, the air velocity will be greater than the speed of the wing through the air, whilst it will be less over the lower surface. This is equivalent to superimposing a vortex on the mainstream velocity, known as the bound vortex. According to a theorem due to Helmholtz, a vortex cannot just end in mid-air, and hence, where the bound vorticity becomes less, a trailing vortex leaves the wing trailing downstream. In general, therefore, a lifting wing will be followed by a system of trailing

11

vortices, the precise nature of which will depend on the spanwise distribution of lift across the wing. These vortices will induce a downward component of velocity at and behind the wing and the downwash at any section of the wing will be the sum of all the effects of the trailing vortices across the span. This downwash, together with the mainstream velocity, rotates the mainstream and hence also rotates the lift vector, giving it a component in the direction of motion. This component is equivalent to a drag and is, in fact the induced drag.

Mathematically, this leads to quite a complicated situation, and the calculation of the induced drag of a wing of given planform is by no means sraightforward. It can be further complicated if the wing has some spanwise twist. If the spanwise lift distribution is elliptical, it can be shown that the induced drag is then a minimum, and the value of the downwash is then constant. Its value will be

$$\varepsilon = C_L \big/ \pi A \ , \tag{2.1}$$

and the induced drag coefficient will then have the value

$$C_{Di} = C_L^2 \big/ \pi A \ . \tag{2.2}$$

For wings with some other lift distribution, the above expression can include a *k* before the right-hand side, *k* being a constant generally greater than 1.0. If we consider the induced drag of planar wings, any variation from the elliptical lift distribution will produce an increase in induced drag, but it is comforting to appreciate that the lift has a distinct tendency to become elliptical. Indeed, Schrenk (1940) devised the approximate rule that the distribution of the lift associated with the untwisted chord distribution is nearly proportional to the ordinate lying halfway between the elliptical and actual chord distributions for the same total area and span. Hence the wing which will produce an elliptical spanwise lift distribution is untwisted and has an elliptical planform. For real wings, an elliptical planform is a great nuisance, because everything has double curvature. It is much simpler to devise a wing whose generators are straight lines, and this can be done in two or three spanwise stages. For a well-designed wing, the increase in drag relative to the "elliptical" value can be very small (Boermans and Waibel,

1989). For sailplane aspect ratios, k will commonly be between 1.02 and 1.05.

Everyone's idea of the perfect elliptical wing is, of course, that of the "Spitfire". But that wing had two degrees of washout (i.e., the tip was twisted two degrees nose-down compared with the root), so the lift distribution was decidedly non-elliptical.

It is important to note that there is no way of escaping induced drag. Ultimately, it is a consequence of Newton's laws, resulting in the application of downwash to the air over a finite span. But it is possible to invest in a non-planar lifting system, with less induced drag than a simple planar wing by using *winglets*. The ultimate non-planar lifting system is, of course, the biplane — even more generally, the multiplane (Prandtl and Teitjens, 1934, para., 119) and it can readily be shown that the total induced drag of a biplane is less than that of a monoplane *of the same span and total lift*. The effect, however, is not very great: if the ratio of the vertical spacing between the wings to the span is 0.2, then the induced drag of the biplane will be about 0.74 times that of the monoplane. An increase in span of the monoplane of about 15% would produce the same effect, or about 2.25 m for a 15 m sailplane. Before rushing off to design the ultimate biplane sailplane, it is important to contemplate the effects of the above restrictions on the overall layout.

It can also be shown (Prandtl and Teitjens, 1934, para., 120) that if it is assumed that all of the downward momentum applied to the air in producing the lift is in the form of a uniform velocity, then this can be imagined as affecting a cylindrical stream tube, whose diameter is equal to the span. All of this applies when the lift distribution is elliptical. This, of course, is a highly artificial way of visualising the actual scene, in which velocities induced by the vortices associated with the wing extend to infinity, but it is a useful way of visualising the scene. It therefore follows that any induced drag reduction can only be achieved by increasing the area of the stream tube. Devices such as winglets do this in the vertical direction to a limited extent (Marsden, 1991), and can reduce the induced drag by about 20%. However, there is some increase in the skin friction, and much of their merit consists of improving the roll rate and decreasing the tip-stalling tendency.

It can be inferred from the above remarks about Schrenk's method that, if a wing has a large amount of taper, the loading will increase towards the tip. This, together with the decreasing Reynolds number in this region, will tend to lead to premature tip stalling. However, this can be discouraged by applying washout, i.e., twisting the wing in the leading edge down, but this obviously changes the spanwise lift distribution usually in the sense of increasing sense the induced drag. Some types of wooden sailplane of a former generation appeared to produce a download over the outer parts of the wing at high speeds, and they could be seen bending downwards quite markedly. Incidentally, the washout does *not* increase linearly with spanwise distance for a wing with straight-line generators.

It will be seen that the downwash at any spanwise station is influenced by the distribution of circulation across the whole span, and the local circulation for a given wing will depend on the downwash. In general, therefore, this situation leads to an integral equation (Kuethe and Chow, 1986, p. 145), for which straightforward solutions only exist for a few special cases. Solutions for the general case were due to Glauert (1937). Computer programs exist for dealing with this situation, but a semi-empirical method is due to Diederich (1952), explained further in Torenbeek (1982), App. E.

Three-Dimensional Lift Curve Slope

A further consequence of the reduction of the wing incidence due to the downwash is a decrease in the lift curve slope. If this has the "elliptical" value of Eq. (2.1), and the two-dimensional lift curve slope is a_o, then the 3-D lift curve slope will be $a_o \pi A /(a_o + \pi A)$. If the 2-D slope is close to 2π, this becomes $a_o A /(A + 2)$. Although this appears to have rather restricted applicability, it is quite accurate in most circumstances.

Drag of Three-Dimensional Wings

For a real wing of finite span in real fluid, there are therefore two sources of drag; the profile drag, which is mentioned in Chapter 1, and the induced drag, as mentioned above. The profile drag is due in the main to skin friction, or to tangential forces on the wing surface, whilst the induced drag is ultimately due to normal pressures acting perpendicularly to the surface. In order to calculate the profile drag of a wing, we assume that, at any spanwise station, the wing section has the same characteristics with respect to the rotated airstream as it has in normal two-dimensional flow. Integration across the span then gives the total profile drag.

Tail surfaces

Tail surfaces are, of course, small wings and therefore all of the above remarks will apply while taking account of elevator deflections. However, it is important to note that the tailplane is exposed to the downwash from both the bound and trailing vortex systems of the wing, whereas in calculating the induced drag of a wing, we consider only the effect of the trailing vortices. Also, in general, the tailplane will have its own induced drag. For a detailed analysis of these matters, see Jones, 1979 and Vernon, 1992.

References

Boermans, L.M.M. and Waibel, G., "Aerodynamic design of the standard class sailplane ASW-24", *Technical Soaring*, XIII, **3**.

Diederich, F.W. "A simple approximate method for calculating spanwise lift distributions and aerodynamic influence coefficients at subsonic speeds", *NACA TN* **2751**, 1952.

Glauert, H., *Elements of Airfoil and Airscrew Theory*, Cambridge University Press, 1937.

Jones, R.T., "Minimising induced drag", *Soaring*, October, 1979.

Kuethe, A.M. and Chow, C.-Y., *Foundations of Aerodynamics*, John Wiley and Sons, 1986.

Marsden, D.J., "Winglets for sailplanes", *Technical Soaring*, XV, **4**.

Prandtl, L. and Teitjens, O.G., *Applied Hydro- and Aeromechanics*, Dover Publications, New York, 1934 and 1957.

Schrenk, O., "Simple approximation method for obtaining spanwise lift distribution", *NACA TM* **948**, 1940.

Torenbeek, E., *Synthesis of Subsonic Airplane Design*, Delft University Press, 1982.

Vernon, C.O., "Trim drag", *Technical Soaring*, XVI, **1**.

Chapter 3

THE DRAG OF A SAILPLANE

Finding the total drag of a sailplane is, strictly speaking, a very complicated matter. It will not simply suffice to add together the drags of the various components, taking into account the induced drags of the wing and tail, remembering that the latter will be working in the induced downwash of the former. To some extent, the performance will depend on the CG position (Irving, 1981, and Vernon, 1992) which, in turn, settles the tail load. So we should, strictly, define the CG position to which the stated performance applies, and then, given a suitable knowledge of static stability, the tail load and the elevator setting can be defined for each lift coefficient. However, in practice, the performance varies little with CG position and it will normally suffice to give it for some average location. It might be thought that some fairly aft position of the CG would be best, since this would normally give the least downwards load on the tailplane, or perhaps a small upwards load at low speeds and, indeed, the tailplane might well be sized so as to make this possible. But as we shall see later, the reality is more complicated. Also, we cannot simply add together the individual drags of the components of the sailplane, because the flow about one part, the wing for example, alters the drag of an adjacent component, in this case the fuselage. It may well be necessary to apply a little CFD to explore the flow about, say, the wing roots. It can well be imagined that when one takes into account the changing aspects of the boundary layer and the interactions hinted at above, then the total drag even in steady flight will be unlikely to conform to a simple analytical expression. In situations where the performance needs to be stated over a wide range of conditions, one may well use a polynomial fitted to the observed performance. For example, Pierson, 1977, assumes a simple quadratic expression while other authors have taken more complicated expressions.

The Parabolic Polar

If we assume that the total drag coefficient of a sailplane may be written

$$C_D = C_{Do} + kC_L^2/\pi A \tag{3.1}$$

where C_{Do} is the minimum drag coefficient of the sailplane, assumed constant, and k is also constant, then if we replace the drag and lift coefficients, as in Eqs. (1.1) and (1.2), we get:

$$WV_{si} = AV_i^3 + B/V_i \tag{3.2}$$

since it is also true that

$$DV_i = WV_{si} \tag{3.3}$$

as we shall see in more detail in Chapter 4.

The expression "parabolic polar" is a consequence of Eq. (3.1), and A and B are likewise constants. Now Fig. 1.1 shows that the profile drag of a wing, and hence of a complete sailplane, is far from constant. But it is not too far from parabolic, provided that the lift coefficient is not too extreme, and hence we can regard (3.1) as being fairly accurate, provided that we recognise that k now includes a contribution from the profile drag. Indeed, if we work back from an actual polar to an expression in the form of (3.1), we find that k is of the order of 1.5, instead of the much lower value to be expected from Chapter 2 (see Goodhart, 1970). It will also be seen that the minimum value of the profile drag is at a slightly positive value of the lift coefficient, instead of zero as assumed in the above expressions. This is equivalent to introducing a term in C_L in Eq. (3.1), but experience shows that such a term is usually unnecessary.

This sort of thinking applies not only to fixed geometry sailplanes, but also to those with flaps, provided that the performance curve now

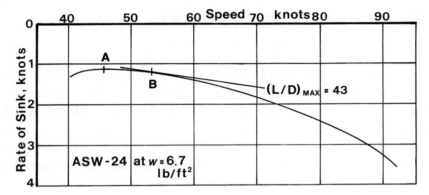

Fig. 3.1. The performance curve or "polar" of the ASW-24 at a wing loading of 6.7 lb per square foot.

represents the envelope of all the curves corresponding to the various flap settings.

What is the reason for wishing to obtain an analytical expression for the performance of a sailplane? Partly because simple expressions can be adduced for best gliding angle, minimum sink, etc., as in the next chapter, and because it enables results for the MacCready ring and similar devices to be obtained without trying to draw tangents. And how accurate is it? Usually pretty good, for speeds a little more than that of the best gliding angle up to about the highest speed likely to be used in practice. Divergence from this simple result is mainly due to turbulent separation at low speeds and laminar separation bubbles at high speeds. See, for example, the performance curve of the ASW-24, in Fig. 3.1.

Significant Speeds

For a sailplane with a parabolic polar, the performance curve will look like Fig. 3.1. The minimum rate of sink will correspond to point A and the best gliding angle to point B. At point A, the equivalent airspeed is:

$$V_{ims} = \left(4kw^2/3\pi A\, C_{Do}\, \rho_o^2\right)^{\frac{1}{4}} \tag{3.4}$$

and the "equivalent" minimum rate of sink is:

$$V_{si\,min} = 4\left(4k^3 C_{Do}\, w^2 / 27\, \pi^3 A^3 \rho_o^2\right)^{\frac{1}{4}} . \qquad (3.5)$$

These rather complicated-looking results can be obtained by assuming that $L = W$, substituting in detail for the quantities in (3.2) above and differentiating to find the minimum value of $V_s(\rho/\rho_o)$. Also, it will be noted that the concept of "equivalent" vertical speeds, analogous to equivalent forward speeds as discussed in Chapter 1, is being introduced here. This has the merit that the value of quantities such as the equivalent minimum rate of sink is independent of height.

Likewise, differentiating to find the least value of V_{si}/V_i gives the speed for best gliding angle as:

$$V_{io} = 3^{\frac{1}{4}} V_{ims} \qquad (3.6)$$

and the best gliding angle will be:

$$\left(V_{si}/V_s\right)_{min} = \tan^{-1}\left(4k\, C_{Do}/\pi A\right)^{\frac{1}{2}} . \qquad (3.7)$$

Rather more familiar will be the maximum lift/drag ratio, whose value will be $(\pi A/4_R C_{Do})$.

At first sight, it might be thought that the quantities corresponding to the symbols above are all truly independent. However, in practice, increasing the aspect ratio, A, will normally increase the wing loading, w, and cause a slight decrease in the "induced drag factor", k. Also, the span, b, does not appear specifically in these equations, and one might be tempted to suppose that a good 1ft span model of, say, an ASH-25, would give the same performance as the real thing with a span of 82 ft, provided that the wing loadings remain the same. This does not occur in practice because the Reynolds number of the real thing is so much higher than that of the model, leading to a far better performance. Also, the best gliding angle and the minimum rate of sink, both decrease as the aspect ratio increases, other things being equal, so one might be tempted to think that the highest possible aspect ratio, limited only by the structure, should be used. This is more-or-less true, if there is no limit to the span, but in the case of a Standard or 15 m Class machine, where the span is fixed, too high an aspect ratio will lead to a wing loading which is inconveniently high for circling in thermals on an average day. To some extent, this can be overcome by carrying water ballast on good days, but it is worth noting that the total weight should be proportional to the square root of the rate of climb, to a first approximation, leading to some spectacular quantities of ballast on really good days. And, so far, we have totally ignored the possibility of flutter, which is often a major consideration in the design of high aspect ratio wings. So, in practice, the various quantities mentioned above are not independent and one must be careful about drawing conclusions from the above equations.

The Non-Parabolic Polar

A polar may not conform to equations such as (3.2), but it remains true that at point A, the drag power will be a minimum, i.e., $dDV/dV = 0$ and at point B, $dD/dV = 0$. It is worth noting that the application of these criteria gives speeds in both cases which, being "true", increase with height. But they can equally be written with V_i substituted for V, in which case, the speeds will be "equivalent" and will not be a function of height. Most of the results which follow apply generally, but can be simplified if the polar is parabolic. It is also true that the speed for best gliding angle is higher than that for minimum sink, which itself is higher than the stalling speed, but in many cases, simple expressions such as (3.6) will not apply. See Miele, 1962, pp. 120–123, for a fuller explanation.

Reynolds Number Effects

Broadly speaking, profile drag coefficients will tend to decrease with increasing Reynolds number. A consequence is that the maximum lift/drag ratio, which appears to be independent of the wing loading, will increase slightly when the weight is increased by the use of ballast. The difference in best gliding angle, as between the unballasted and fully ballasted conditions, may well be of the order of one unit. If we compare conditions at the same equivalent airspeed, taking heights of sea-level and 10,000 ft, we find that the Reynolds number at the greater height is about 10% less. (There are two effects, one due to the effect of density, and the other due to viscosity, both of which can be obtained from tables of the Standard Atmosphere.) This is to be compared with an increase of about 15% in Reynold's number due to the ballast in a typical case.

A Note on the Analytical Polar

Equation (3.2) above implies that the complete polar can be defined from a knowledge of just two quantities, the constants A and B. This is only strictly true of sailplanes having parabolic polars and fixed geometry, but it will not be greatly in error for the more generalised shape of polar, taking the optimum envelope for flapped sailplanes. This enables optimisation calculations, as in Chapter 9, to be greatly simplified.

References

Goodhart, H.C.N., "A note on the measurement of the induced drag factor (k) of a glider", *OSTIV Publication* **XI**, 1970.

Irving, F.G., "The optimum centre of gravity position for minimum overall energy loss", *OSTIY Publication* **XVI**, 1981.

Miele, A., *Flight Mechanics, Vol. I, Theory of Flight Paths*, Pergamon, 1962.

Pierson, B.L., "Sailplane winch-launch trajectories", *Aeronautical Quarterly*, May, 1977.

Vernon, C.O., "Trim drag", *Technical Soaring*, January, 1992.

Chapter 4

THE EQUATIONS OF MOTION

The General Equations of Motion for Flight in a Vertical Plane

Here, we will only be concerned with the relatively slow motions of an aircraft, with typical times in minutes, so that we can confine our attention to the force equations only. The more rapid motions, with a timescale of seconds, are the province of stability and the moment equations. For the present, we will consider symmetrical flight in a vertical plane (turning flight is considered later), so only two of the force equations are relevant. We also assume that:

1. The thrust vector (if present, as in motor gliders) lies in the plane of symmetry of the sailplane.
2. In steady straight flight with the wings level, the plane of symmetry is vertical and contains the resultant velocity vector.
3. We take axes Ox, Oy, Oz whose origin is at the centre of mass (or centre of gravity, CG). Ox lies along the direction of motion, in the plane of symmetry and Oz is perpendicular to Ox, also in the plane of symmetry and directed downwards for a sailplane in normal flight. Oy is directed to starboard. These form a right-handed set of axes, strictly known as "air path axes" or, less formally, as "wind axes".
4. The local slope of the flight path, and hence of Ox, is denoted by Γ, and the velocity along Ox by V. By definition, there will be no velocity component along Oz.
5. The implication of para., 3 and 4 above is that Ox is not fixed in direction relative to a datum line inscribed on the sailplane. For example, if the datum is the zero-lift line, the angle between it and Ox will be α, which will vary with the conditions of flight. Since we

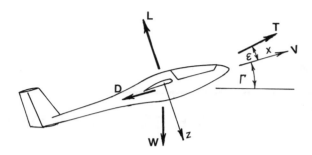

Fig. 4.1. The forces acting on a motor glider in symmetrical flight. For a pure sailplane, the thrust is omitted.

are only concerned with the force equations, this does not matter, but it is worth noting that, in considering the stability, we must use an axis system fixed in relative to the airframe.

It is also assumed that the thrust acts at an angle ε to Ox, which will normally be small. Also, if the axis system has an angular velocity q about the centre of curvature of the flight path, there will be an acceleration $-V^2/R$, or $-Vq$ along Oz. Since q is the rate of change of flight path slope, $d\Gamma/dt$, this component of acceleration can finally be written $-V(d\Gamma/dt)$. The general state of affairs is, therefore, as shown in Fig. 4.1.

Since force = mass × acceleration, the equations of motion become:

$$-mg\sin\Gamma - D + T\cos\varepsilon = m\,dV/dt \qquad (4.1)$$

$$mg\cos\Gamma - L - T\sin\varepsilon = -mV\left(d\Gamma/dt\right) \qquad (4.2)$$

along Ox and Oz respectively.

Simplifications

In steady flight, $dV/dt = d\Gamma/dt = 0$. Also, ε is often taken to be zero. With these conditions inserted, these equations become:

$$-mg\sin\Gamma - D + T = 0 \qquad (4.3)$$

$$mg \cos \Gamma - L = 0 \tag{4.4}$$

and if $T = 0$, in other words if we have a pure sailplane, Eq. (4.3) becomes simply

$$-mg \sin \Gamma - D = 0. \tag{4.5}$$

Remarks on These Equations

If we divide (4.5) by (4.4), we get:

$$\tan \Gamma = -D/L \tag{4.6}$$

which indicates that in steady flight, Γ will be negative, a consequence of the conventional system of axes shown in Fig. 4.1. Also, Γ willl normally be small, and there will be very little difference between Γ, $\tan \Gamma$ and $\sin \Gamma$, if Γ is in radians. It is worth noting that in the case of the space shuttle, Γ, in the landing phase, is no longer small and there will be a significant difference between the exact and approximate expressions. If we square and add Eqs. (4.4) and (4.5), we get:

$$mg = \left(L^2 + D^2 \right)^{\frac{1}{2}}. \tag{4.7}$$

This indicates that, in steady flight, the weight is equal to the resultant aerodynamic force acting on the sailplane, the result to be expected from Fig. 4.2.

If we multiply Eq. (4.5) by V and put $mg = W$, we get

$$-WV \sin \Gamma - DV = 0, \tag{4.8}$$

and if we put $-V \sin \Gamma = V_s$, the rate of sink, then (4.8) becomes

$$WV_s = DV \tag{4.9}$$

as one might expect from the conservation of energy. If we multiply both sides of this equation by $(\sigma)^{\frac{1}{2}}$, we arrive at the result quoted in Eq. (3.3).

So far, all of the results quoted in this chapter apply whether the polar is parabolic or not.

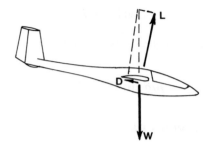

Fig. 4.2. In steady flight, the weight of a pure sailplane is balanced by the resultant aerodynamic force.

Results for a Parabolic Polar

Equation (3.2) was

$$WV_{si} = AV_i^3 + B/V_i,$$

and differentiating this expression shows that the glide angle, now assumed to be (V_{si}/V_i), will be a minimum at an equivalent airspeed V_{io}, where

$$V_{io} = (B/A)^{\frac{1}{4}}. \qquad (4.10)$$

The corresponding rate of sink will be V_{sio}, where

$$WV_{sio} = 2(AB^3)^{\frac{1}{4}}. \qquad (4.11)$$

Combining these three expressions, Eq. (3.2) may therefore be written in dimensionless terms as follows:

$$2V_{si}/V_{sio} = (V_i/V_{io})^3 + (V_{io}/V_i), \qquad (4.12)$$

which again shows that we only need to know two quantities, in this case the equivalent speed for maximum L/D ratio and the corresponding equivalent rate of sink to define the whole polar. In other words, all polars are basically of the same shape but can be stretched horizontally or vertically, as appropriate. If we know V_{sio} and V_{io}, these can be substituted in (4.12) to get the dimensional polar.

Also, if these quantities are known for a weight W_1 and we wish to find the polar for weight W_2, then they can simply be multiplied by $(W_2/W_1)^{\frac{1}{2}}$ (neglecting the effect of Reynolds number), which implies that a considerable amount of ballast is required to make a significant difference to the polar. The same is also true for the envelope of polars corresponding to optimum flap settings for a flapped sailplane.

This, of course, is not exactly true of real polars, but something close to it still holds. The object of having a dimensionless curve will become apparent in Chapter 8, where the optimisation of flight in thermals will be discussed.

Best speeds for Motor Sailplanes

In the cases of self-launching or self-sustaining motor sailplanes, we will be mainly interested in the maximum rate of climb and the corresponding speed. This will occur when the drag is a minimum, assuming that with a fixed-pitch propeller, its efficiency is at a maximum at this speed, in other words, at a speed for best gliding angle. It is worth noting, however, that deploying the propeller causes a large increment in drag, thus increasing the speed for maximum L/D, as indicated by Eqs. (3.5) and (3.6). Likewise, the steepest angle of climb will correspond to the minimum drag-power speed, the speed for minimum rate of sink, again assuming that the propeller efficiency is now a maximum at this speed. With a fixed-pitch propeller, it clearly cannot have a maximum efficiency at both speeds, and it would be better to aim for the best rate of climb rather than the best angle of climb.

Performance in Turning Flight

So far, we have only considered straight flight, in which the components of weight along Ox, Oy and Oz axes were $-mg \sin\Gamma$, 0, and $mg \cos\Gamma$. If we now visualize the sailplane of Fig. 4.1 rolled about Ox through an angle Φ, and we are looking along the Ox axis, then Fig. 4.3 portrays what happens. The components of weight along the three axes now become $-mg \sin\Gamma$, $mg \cos\Gamma \sin\Phi$ and $mg \cos\Gamma \cos\Phi$. As before,

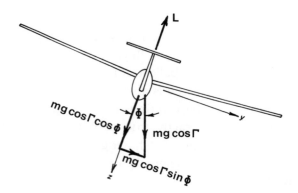

Fig. 4.3. The sailplane of Fig. 4.1 rolled about the Ox axis. Note that the Ox axis is not horizontal.

there will be an acceleration $-Vq$ along Oz, but now we must also take into account an angular velocity r about Oz, so that, finally, the components of acceleration along the axes are 0, Vr and $-Vq$. If the sailplane has an angular velocity Ω about a vertical axis, then:

$$q = \Omega \cos \Gamma \sin \Phi \qquad (4.13)$$

and

$$r = \Omega \cos \Gamma \cos \Phi , \qquad (4.14)$$

since the components of Ω are analogous to those of g.

The equations of motion, which were (4.1) and (4.2) in straight flight, now become:

$$- mg \sin \Gamma - D + T \cos \varepsilon = m dV/dt \qquad (4.15)$$

$$mg \cos \Gamma \sin \Phi = mV r = mV \Omega \cos \Gamma \cos \Phi \qquad (4.16)$$

$$mg \cos \Gamma \cos \Phi - L - T \sin \varepsilon = - mV \Omega \cos \Gamma \sin \Phi \qquad (4.17)$$

along the Ox, Oy and Oz axes respectively.

These equations are included here for the sake of completeness. If, as before, we assume steady flight, then $dV/dt = 0$; for a pure sailplane

$T = 0$, and if the glide angle is flat $\Gamma \sim 0$. Then these equations simplify to:

$$-mg \sin \Gamma - D = 0 \qquad (4.18)$$

$$V\Omega/g = \tan \Phi \qquad (4.19)$$

$$mg \cos \Phi - L = -mV\Omega \sin \Phi \,. \qquad (4.20)$$

It then follows from Eqs. (4.19) and (4.20) that:

$$n = L/W = \sec \Phi \qquad (4.21)$$

and Eq. (4.19) is conveniently written

$$R = V^2/g \tan \Phi \,. \qquad (4.22)$$

Now Fig. 3.1 shows a typical performance curve in straight flight, at a load factor L/W of unity. A point on this curve will correspond to a given lift coefficient so, if the load factor when circling is n, the forward speed at the same lift coefficient will be increased by $n^{\frac{1}{2}}$ from Eq. (1.1). Since the lift/drag ratio at a given lift coefficient is constant, the drag will be multiplied by n, and it follows from Eq. (4.9) that the rate of sink will be multiplied by $n^{3/2}$. Finally, from Eq. (4.21):

$$V_\phi/V_1 = \left(\sec \Phi \right)^{1/2} \qquad (4.23)$$

$$V_\phi/V_{s1} = \left(\sec \Phi \right)^{3/2} \,. \qquad (4.24)$$

So the effect of angle of bank on turning performance will be as shown, for a typical case, as in Fig. 4.4.

It will not have escaped the astute reader that this is all very well, but it assumes that, apart from the additional loading, everything is as in straight flight. Clearly, this is not true: when turning steadily, the outer wing, on the average will have a higher speed than the inner wing, and there will, therefore, be a rolling moment tending to roll the sailplane into the turn. This means that the pilot must apply an aileron deflection to oppose this rolling momentum in the "holding off bank" sense, which means an increase in profile drag due to the aileron deflection. Also, the

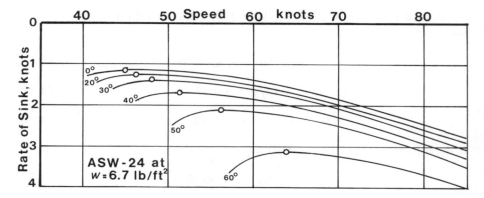

Fig. 4.4. The effect of angle of bank on the performance of the sailplane of Fig. 3.1.

trailing vortices are now more-or-less helical, as opposed to trailing straight behind the sailplane, which will tend to increase the induced drag. This has been investigated by Phillips (1972), who concluded that the latter effect was negligble, being less than 2% under the most adverse circumstances considered.

The increase in profile drag will depend on the characteristics of individual wing sections, and in general, on separation of the flow over the upper surface of the down-going aileron. If this condition can be avoided, the increase in profile drag coefficient will also be very small. These effects can be reduced by shifting the CG laterally, a somewhat unlikely procedure. There will also be a further increase in profile drag, because the fuselage, etc., is also in a curved flow.

Figure 4.5 shows the rate of sink plotted against radius of turn, for various angles of bank, as deduced from Fig. 4.4 and Eq. (4.22), the use of which will be apparent in Chapter 8.

Ground Effect

When a finite wing is near the ground, it experiences less down-wash than in free flight. There are two ways of looking at this phenomenon: the downwash cannot pass through the solid earth, which causes a reduction in the downwash when the height is small;

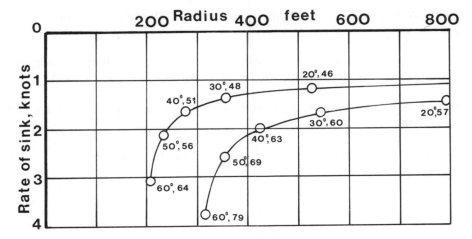

Fig. 4.5. The minimum sink of the sailplane of Fig. 3.1 at various angles of bank and for two wing loadings. The upper curve applies to a wing loading of 6.7 lb per square foot whilst the lower applies to 10.2 lb per square foot. Beside each point, the first figure is the angle of bank, the second the airspeed for minimum rate of sink.

alternatively, a wing close to the ground is equivalent to having an imaginary mirror-image wing below the ground, with the real wing working in the upwash due to the latter. Half-way between the two, the streamlines must be straight, due to symmetry. This leads to two effects: the lift curve slope is increased and the induced drag coefficient is reduced. The first effect depends on the ratio h/b, i.e., the height divided by the span, and on the aspect ratio, whilst the second depends largely on h/b alone. The increase in lift curve slope is probably not very noticeable to the pilot, but the decrease in induced drag can be significant. An 80 ft span wing 10 ft up will have about 60% of the induced drag of the same wing in free flight.

References

Most of this chapter is taken, with suitable revisions for sailplanes, from from the author's lecture notes in aircraft performance, at Imperial College. Also see:

Welch, A. & L. and Irving, F.G., *New Soaring Pilot*, Third Edition, John Murray, 1977.

Phillips, W.H., "Analysis of the effect of asymmetric loading on sailplane performance in circling flight", *NASA Contractor Report CR-2315*, 1973.

Kuethe, A.M. and Chow, C-Y., *Foundations of Aerodynamics*, John Wiley and Sons, 1986.

Hoerner, S.F., *Fluid-Dynamic* Drag, published by the Author, 1965.

SECTION B:
INSTRUMENTS FOR SOARING FLIGHT

Chapter 5

INSTRUMENTS FOR SOARING FLIGHT

The Variometer and Similar Devices

As will be seen in Chapter 8, both the vertical speed and the speed along the flight path need to expressed similarly: in other words, both should be either "true" or both should be "equivalent". In fact, the latter represents the simpler arrangement, since a single performance curve then applies at all heights. However, at an elementary level, it is almost inevitable that there will be a mismatch, but under most circumstances, the effect will be negligible.

Kronfeld, advised by Lippisch (Welch, 1965), is generally thought to have been the first to use a variometer, and it contributed greatly to his success in competitions in 1930. The actual device was probably of the "Badin" type, originally developed for ballooning, not greatly different from the present day "Winter" or "PZL" types. In these instruments, a vane is mounted on a horizontal shaft, slightly off-centre, so that the gap between the vane and the case increases with increasing deflection. The indicating hand is mounted on the end of the shaft and a centralising spring is fitted. One side of the vane is connected to a capacity and the other to the static pressure or a total energy device. Clearly, such an instrument has to be built to very exacting standards and fitted with remarkable bearings, since the rate of flow of air through the instrument is very small indeed. It is, therefore, surprising to find that such a simple device shows almost exactly the "true" rate of climb or sink and, indeed, on powered aeroplanes, the Vertical Speed Indicator is carefully "tweaked" by suitable restrictions in its connections to the outside world, to ensure

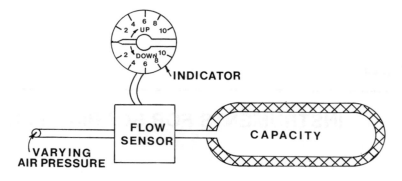

Fig. 5.1. The basic circuit diagram of a variometer.

that any errors are negligible. The basic circuit diagram for any variometer is as shown in Fig. 5.1.

Total Energy

The whole concept of total energy now seems so obvious that it is surprising, in retrospect, that it was not considered earlier. To the best of my knowledge, it was first mentioned in print (in the context of soaring) in a letter by Arthur Kantrowitz and printed in the Journal of the Aeronautical Sciences, dated 4th September 1940. It is worth reproducing in full, with source minor typological changes to suit the computer, suice it explains the principles so well.

"Dear Sir:

In soaring, a rate of climb meter (variometer) is usually used to detect upward currents in the atmosphere. The rate of climb of a sailplane is, however, dependent upon *two* things: first the atmospheric currents and the drag (or sinking speed) and second, the plane's attitude. It is necessary, therefore, to discount the second effect, i.e., the effect of diving or zooming before information about atmospheric currents can be obtained from a variometer. This is a difficult procedure in flight since the atmosphere is usually rough during favorable soaring conditions. The object of this note is to present a variometer arrangement in which zooming or diving is corrected for automatically.

When a sailplane is zooming or diving, it is gaining or losing altitude energy at the expense of kinetic energy. It is, however, changing its total energy (altitude energy + kinetic energy) at a rate which depends only on its drag and atmospheric air currents. Thus, if we measure the rate of change of total energy instead of just altitude energy, we have a measurement of atmospheric currents and sinking speed independent of the plane's attitude. Further, the total energy is the quantity in which the soaring pilot is interested in increasing. The total energy of a plane of mass m, flying at a velocity v at an altitude h is

$$\tfrac{1}{2} m v^2 + mgh$$

and it is thus proportional to $\tfrac{1}{2} v^2 + gh$.

In the usual design, the atmospheric outlet of the variometer is connected to the static head where it is exposed to the altitude pressure $-\rho g h$ (ρg is the density, h the altitude, and pressure is measured from sea level pressure). Now, consider the variometer outlet to be connected to the throat of a venturi with a contraction ratio of $2^{\frac{1}{2}}$ which will produce a pressure drop equal to the dynamic pressure $\tfrac{1}{2} \rho V^2$. A venturi tube was suggested to Mr E. N. Jacobs to produce the pressure drop because it is relatively insensitive to angle of attack. In this case, the variometer will be exposed to a pressure

$$-\rho g h - \tfrac{1}{2} \rho v^2 \,.$$

Thus, this negative pressure is also proportional to $\tfrac{1}{2} v^2 + gh$ which is just the measure of the sailplane's total reserve of energy. Therefore, if a conventional variometer were connected in this manner, it would read rate of change of total energy in altitude units. A variometer so connected may be called a "total energy variometer". With a total energy variometer, it should be possible to measure upward air currents, even in rough air when the attitude of the ship is continually changing, without making any corrections.

Arthur Kantrowitz
National Advisory Committee for Aeronautics"

August Raspet (Barringer, 1942, Chap. VII) had clearly read this letter and proposed a venturi with a contraction ratio of 0.7106, but it is doubtful whether it was flown.

In Europe, at any rate, there were other things to be done in 1940 and there the matter rested until early 1952 (Kendall, 1952), when the matter was revived. Hugh Kendall's system used bulges on the fuselage sides to provide the suction and, since he said he had not read Kantrowitz, this made his design a remarkable invention. This arrangment suffered from the drawback that, due to local changes in the curvature of wooden fuselages, every installation had to be individually calibrated. At about the same time, I produced a different device, with the suction provided by a venturi as suggested by Kantrowitz (whom I hadn't read, either), although I did know about Hugh Kendall's experiments. This had the advantage that, having settled on the proportions of the venturi, that was the end of the calibration process. (Irving, 1952). The venturi was of quite a complex shape: downstream of the throat, there was a sudden enlargement in the bore, so that one could be a little more carefree than Kantrowitz in selecting the minimum diameter, and at its rear end there was an external disc to reduce its sensitivity to yaw (Irving, 1952). To this day, there are pirated mini-versions of this tube being made in Germany. The external disc was borrowed from a German wartime idea, so the whole thing was something of a pastiche. This was the British team's "secret weapon" — a phrase which was still popular at the time — for the 1952 World Championships and two machines were suitably equipped, one with Hugh Kendall's device and another with mine. As it happened, we won the championship, and Philip Wills later wrote "…the most important advance in recent years is in the refinement of the variometer" (Wills, 1952).

There matters rested, in gliding at any rate, until 1955 when a totally different device was invented (Vogeli, 1955) where the total energy effect was obtained by means of a diaphragm pressurized by the pitot, so that increasing pitot pressure effectively decreased the size of the capacity. Whilst this was entirely internal, it suffered from the problem that its calibration did indeed vary with height (Irving, 1956), although, as usual a single device worked quite well over an appreciable range of height.

Since there are relatively few about, we will not indulge in a detailed description.

Then somebody in Germany noted that the pressure coefficient on the downstream side of a circular cylinder at Reynolds numbers of about 10,000 is quite close to -1.0 (Goldstein, 1938), leading to a device incorrectly called the Braunschweig Tube. The tube had two slots on its downstream side, subtending a total angle of $110°$ at its centre with its end perpendicular to the airflow. This was all very well except that a small slip with the saw could appreciably alter the entire pressure coefficient. Also, there is a marked end effect, not covered in the original tests.

In 1976, a further improvement occurred (Nicks, 1976). The final tube was now at an angle of 70% to the flow and a single 1/16" hole was located 3/8" from the end of the 3/16" tube. At the same time, I was conducting rather similar experiments at Imperial College, which indicated that the "Braunschweig" tube produced about 11% too much suction and Oran Nicks' about 12% too little (Irving, 1978). It is only fair to say that the original Nicks tube was not exactly replicated, so these results may not be quite correct. In my tube, assisted by a student, we tracked down the positions at which the trailing vortices separated from the tip, and provided two appropriately located holes.

Here, there was a total angle of $100°$ between the holes, which were 1/16" in diameter and 3/8" from the end of a 1/4" tube. (See Fig. 5.2.) The results were very good indeed, and such tubes have been in production ever since. Incidentally, the point with the 70% tube was that it behaved approximately symmetrically to both positive and negative changes of incidence. Again, numerous pirated versions are in circulation, few of which ever seem to have seen a wind tunnel.

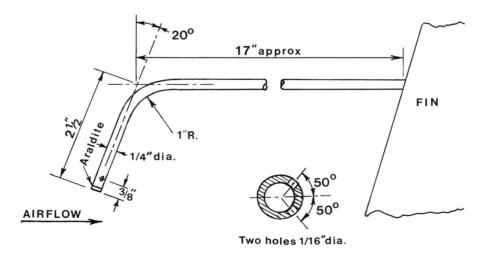

Fig. 5.2. A total-energy head.

While the gliding end of Total Energy was progressing happily, the chaps thinking about supersonic aeroplanes were not exactly idle; probably the first "official" mention in the UK was by Lush (1951). In the US, there were numerous documents: quite a good one, if you are thinking of programming a flight in Concorde, is Meile and Cappellari, 1959.

There is rather more to Total Energy than might be thought from Kantrowitz's letter. If we consider Eq. (4.1), then if we multiply it by V and put $T = 0$, we get:

$$-mgV \sin\Gamma - DV = mV \, dV/dt .$$ (5.1)

Now $V \sin\Gamma$ is the rate of climb, db/dt (remembering that Γ is positive in the nose-up sense), so we get:

$$-DV = mg \, db/dt + \tfrac{1}{2} m \, dV^2/dt$$ (5.2)

or

$$-DV = mg\left(db_e/dt\right).$$ (5.3)

Here, h_e is the "Energy Height", $h + V^2/2g$, i.e., the Total Energy expressed in height terms, corresponding to Kantrowitz's definition. This expression means that its rate of change depends on the drag power, whether or not we are concerned with steady flight. Also, since the polar of a sailplane is, in effect, a plot of DV against V, it is really a curve of rate of change of total energy, the load factor in this case being substantially unity.

Kantrowitz's letter may not have made the description of the total energy variometer entirely clear. If a sailplane is flying at a steady speed in still air, a variometer connected to the static pressure source will show a steady rate of sink. If the pilot now causes the speed to vary by, say, 5 knots on either side of the mean speed, the variometer will show a varying rate of descent. As the speed increases or decreases, the rate of descent will increase or decrease, due to the interchange of kinetic and potential energies. With a total energy variometer, when the speed is increasing, the static pressure increases more rapidly than when flying at a steady speed, but the suction, $-\frac{1}{2}\rho V^2$, is also increasing and cancels out the augmented rate of increase of static pressure p_s. When flying at or near the minimum drag power speed, i.e., near the speed for minimum rate of sink, this cancelling process will be nearly exact, and the variometer will show something very close to the rate of sink at the mean speed. From Eq. (5.3), the variometer will show the rate of change of energy height at any speed, but the effect of variations in speed will become rather more marked as the speed increases simply because the drag has increased. It is often thought that a "perfect" total energy variometer will show an unchanged reading during a sharp pull-up, but not so. The increased load factor will produce a corresponding increase in drag, and hence the variometer will show a temporary increase in rate of sink.

There is, in fact, an error in Kantrowitz's letter, where he refers to "the altitude pressure $-\rho gh$". Now the local atmospheric pressure is not as he states, but it is true that $dp_s = -\rho g dh$. This cannot be integrated to give $p_s = -\rho gh$, because ρ is itself a function of h. However, the variometer deals with the rate of change of pressure, not the actual pressure so, as it happens, this mistake has no effect on the final outcome.

Finally, it follows from all of the above that h_e is the maximum height which would be attained if, at any instant, the sailplane were pointed vertically upwards, neglecting drag.

It also follows from Eq. (5.3) that it is simply not worth having a variometer dealing with normal static pressure, since in normal flight, we are never interested in rates of change of true height. The only exception to this would be if we desire to safeguard the total-energy probe from getting iced up.

In all of the foregoing, we have implicitly assumed that the local air density is constant. More generally, if we seek to determine $d(p_s - \frac{1}{2}\rho V^2)/dt$, which is what a variometer does although the process may be disguised in various ways, there is an additional term $-\frac{1}{2}V^2\,d\rho/dt$, which may be shown to have the approximate value $0.57\,M^2\,dh/dt$ in the troposphere. The constant increases to 0.70 in the stratosphere, where M is the Mach number (Welch and Irving, 1977). Since sailplane Mach numbers rarely exceed 0.2, this term is negligible and, in any case, the total energy sensor would probably produce rather greater errors in the presence of significant Mach numbers.

Electric Variometers

To the best of my knowledge, electric variometers were first mentioned by August Raspet (Barringer, 1942), but the first practical type was devised by P.G. Davey *et al.* at Cambridge University (Davey, 1960), the original problem being to avoid the inevitable inertia, both mechanical and aerodynamic, of the mechanical device. In fact, the problem with the early specimens was to make them less sensitive: they tended to respond to a door being opened at the other end of the building.

The response of most variometer systems will be exponential. If the rate of sink, initially zero, instantly becomes V_s, then, t seconds later, the indication of the variometer will be something like:

$$V_{s\,\text{ind}} = V_s \left[1 - \exp\left(-t/T\right)\right]. \tag{5.4}$$

Here, T is a time constant for the system and is typically about 3.5 sec for a mechanical system. The implication of this equation is that the instrument will never actually read the true value of V_s, but the pilot's impression of the lag will be something like the time taken for the indication to show say 90% of the final V_s. This time is about 2.3 T, or around 8 sec for the mechanical system. Some of this is due to heat transfer effects within the capacity, which can be reduced by filling it with loosely packed non-corrodible wire wool which, although of negligible volume compared with that of the air, will have a large relative heat capacity. The temperature thus stays almost constant as the pressure changes.

A reasonable electric system can be made with a time constant of 0.5 to 1.0 sec: anything less and it starts to display irrelevant 'noise', thus confusing the pilot. Indeed, it will often be necessary to increase the natural time-constant of the electrical device, by inserting a short length of capillary tube in series with the transducer. For example, if the capacity has a volume of $420 \, \text{cm}^3$ and the capillary has a bore of 0.02", then the time constant will be increased by about 1 second per inch of capillary at sea-level. The time constant is inversely proportional to the fourth power of the bore.

The simplest type of electric variometer uses a pair of thermistors in a pipe connected to a flask and heated by passing an electric current through them. Thermistors have a large negative coefficient of resistance and hence, if there is a flow into or out of the flask, the upstream thermistor will be cooled more than the downstream thermistor and its resistance will accordingly be greater. If the thermistors are incorporated in a Wheatstone bridge and the output is suitably amplified, the final output will indicate both the magnitude and direction of the flow. In practice, a modern electric variometer is considerably more complicated than this model suggests, but the general principle is much the same. It is clear that the obstruction experienced by the flow will be markedly less than in a mechanical variometer, there are no moving parts and, since the final output is an electrical signal, it is easy to manipulate it so as to work a second indicator, to give the average over a desired length of time, and use it in the manner suggested in Chapter 8. Also, whereas a mechanical variometer tends to display something very close to the true vertical speed, an electrical instrument shows (true vertical speed) $\times \rho^n$, where n is an index between 0.8 and 1.2. Hence, the output of an electric variometer will also require some adjustment to indicate "equivalent" vertical speed.

There is also a type of variometer which does not require a capacity. In this case, the atmospheric pressure is determined by a suitable transducer, and its output is differentiated electrically to give rate of climb or sink. All electrical instruments can be made to display rate of change of energy height by connecting them to a source of $p_s - \frac{1}{2}\rho V^2$, but in some cases, the total energy input is arranged electrically and no special head is required.

Air Mass Movement

It is also possible to arrange for a variometer to display air mass movement, by subtracting something close to the rate of sink of the sailplane at the prevailing speed from the variometer indication, thus conferring an advantage explained in Chapter 9. This process can be taken even further: to anticipate somewhat, the sailplane should be flown at a particular speed, depending on the circumstances such as rate of sink of the air mass and the strength of the thermals. It is possible to arrange a variometer to display simply whether the sailplane is being flown at the correct speed and, if not, whether the machine should be flown faster or slower.

References

Barringer, L.B., "Flight without power", Pitman Publishing Corporation, 1942.

Davey, P.G., "The electric variometer", *OSTIV Publication* **VI**, 1960.

Goldstein, S. (Ed.), *Modern Developments in Fluid Dynamics*, Clarendon Press, Oxford, 1938. (Reprinted by Dover, New York, 1965). p. 424.

Kendall, H., "The total energy variometer", *Gliding, III*, **1**, Spring 1952.

Irving, F.G., "The total energy variometer", *Gliding, III*, **2**, Summer 1952.

Irving, F.G., "The total energy venturi", *Gliding III*, **4**, Winter, 1952–53.

Irving, F.G., "A total energy variometer operated by pitot pressure", *OSTIV Publication* **IV**, 1958 (Paper originally published in 1956).

Irving, F.G., "A new total energy head", *Sailplane and Gliding XXIX*, **1**, Feb–Mar., 1978.

Lush, K., A Review of the problem of choosing a climb technique, with proposals for a new climb technique for high performance aircraft. *British Aeronautical Research Council R & M*, **2557**, HMSO 1951.

Miele, A. and Cappellari, J.O., "Approximate solutions to optimum flight trajectories for a turbo-jet powered aircraft", *NASA Tech Note* **152**, Sept. 1959.

Nicks, O., "A simple total energy sensor", *Soaring*, Sept. 1976.

Vogeli, E., "Totalenergievariometer", Schweizer Aero Revue, **3**, 1955, p. 91.

Welch A. & L., *The Story of Gliding*, John Murray, London, 1965, Chap. 10.

Welch A. & L. and Irving, F.G., *The New Soaring Pilot*, John Murray, London, 1977, p. 286.

Wills, P.A.W., "The 1952 world championships", *Gliding III*, **3**, Autumn, 1952.

Chapter 6

OTHER INSTRUMENTS

General

For all sailplanes, JAR-22 requires that they carry an airspeed indicator and an altimeter. For powered sailplanes, a magnetic direction indicator is also required and in addition, an accelerometer in fully-aerobatic sailplanes. These, in effect, represent the minimum instrumentation for safe flight but at present Belgium and France also require a variometer, a magnetic direction indicator and a sideslip indicator for all sailplanes. These last amount to National Variations and at the time of writing there is a strong tendency to remove them. This is not the place to debate whether the job of JAR-22 is to define the minimum instrumentation required for safe flight, or what is required to make a sailplane a viable soaring device, but in the present context it is clear that we require at least an ASI, an altimeter, and a variometer so that soaring flight can be conducted to the best effect. The variometer has been considered in the last chapter, and further detail is added in chapter 8. Here we will consider the other instruments.

The Altimeter

The ordinary panel instrument consists of an absolute pressure gauge with a variable datum, calibrated so as to show height in a Standard Atmosphere. This device, when calibrated in English (or American) units, is a very satisfactory instrument, since the largest hand shows 1000 ft per turn: a most satisfactory sensitivity. Here, we should spare a thought for the poor unfortunates who have to deal with metric instruments: either one has 1000 m per turn, which is far too coarse, or

500 m per turn, which tends to lead to ambiguities when heights such as 1740 m are involved.

Normally, an altimeter is coupled to the aircraft's static source and for all practical purposes gives height above the datum in a Standard Atmosphere. If it were coupled to the total energy source, it would give "energy height" but this seems a complication leading to needless ambiguities. There are times when it would be useful to have it set with its datum at 1013.2 mb, to define the heights of controlled airspace, etc. Short of having a second altimeter, which would be rather difficult given the restricted panel space of the average sailplane, the best one can do is to make a note of the datum setting and set its datum to 1013.2 mb when required. This not totally academic, since the height of the bottom of controlled airspace can vary by several hundreds of feet.

There are other methods of defining height. (Incidentally, is it not remarkable that whilst JAR-22 mentions a *magnetic* direction indicator, it does not specify the method of operating the altimeter?) Most electrical final glide indicators will use a transducer to provide the height signal, as doubtless do the electric barographs. And most GPS devices give a height indication relative to some fixed datum, a matter of geometry rather than atmospheric pressure, and not very reliable. The pressure instrument seems likely to be with us for some time.

The Airspeed Indicator

The standard panel instrument is a differential pressure gauge, one side of which is connected to the pitot source, subjected to a pressure $p_s + \frac{1}{2}\rho V^2$, and the other to the static p_s. The difference, in an ideal world, is thus the "dynamic" head, which is easily converted into speed units at sea level in a Standard Atmosphere. However, this is not a perfect world and our instruments will suffer from "pressure" or "position" error. Broadly speaking, the pitot should not suffer from such errors, unless it is faired into the nose or located in the wake of a total energy tube. The static source will often suffer from an error, although this is often small. It is because the static source is usually a pair of small holes in the fuselage, mounted symmetrically on opposite sides so that the effects of small amounts of sideslip is cancel out: but they will rarely convey exactly the local static pressure, simply because the presence of the fuselage itself and other parts of the sailplane tend to produce slight errors.

The total pressure error can be measured by connecting a second ASI across a pitot of undisputed accuracy and a trailing static. The latter usually consists of a glass-fibre cone about 12" in diameter on the end of an 80 ft plastic pipe, about 5/16" or 3/8" in diameter so that it trails well clear of the sailplane. The static holes are drilled in a section of tubing about 3 ft upstream of the cone in an axially symmetrical fashion, the diameter of this piece of tubing being the same as that of the plastic pipe. The sailplane takes off with the trailing static already deployed, which is markedly more convenient than filling the cockpit with tubing, and the whole thing is jettisoned before landing, the cone being light enough to avoid significant damage. This is markedly more convenient than the older bomb-like device. The error is obtained by comparing the aircraft and trailing static ASI's, remembering to calibrate both instruments beforehand.

Jar-22 specifies that the Flight Manual must contain a curve of Equivalent Airspeed as a function of Indicated Airspeed and the maximum difference between the two must not exceed ± 8 km/h or $\pm 5\%$, whichever is greater, throughout the speed range 1.2 V_s to V_{NE} with the wing flaps neutral and airbrakes closed. Now the various design speeds, such as V_D, are expressed in terms of EAS, but the corresponding flight speeds must be expressed in terms of IAS. Thus, if the design dive speed V_D is 150 knots (EAS), then the Demonstrated Dive Speed must lie between 1.0 and 0.9 times V_D, i.e., between 150 and 135 knots EAS. Now suppose that the EAS exceeds the IAS by 5 knots at such speeds and the courageous test pilot takes the sailplane to 142 knots IAS. Then his EAS will have been 147 knots. However, V_{NE} must not exceed 0.9 times V_{DF}, or 132.3 knots EAS. This then becomes 127.3 knots IAS, which would actually be rounded down to 127 knots.

In practice, this rule seems to be fairly widely misunderstood: many current machines have at least two pairs of static holes, and it would indeed be surprising if they both had the same pressure error. Nevertheless, there is only one curve published in the Flight Manual.

Similarly, a remarkable array of sailplanes seem to have never-exceed speeds of 135 knots IAS, and indeed the ASI is colour coded to indicate this. However, it is worth saying that some current sailplanes have negligible pressure errors.

Effect on Best Speeds to Fly

If the pressure errors are significant then the calculations of Chapters 8 to 11 should be carried out in terms of EAS. For example, if the polar is stated in terms of IAS, it should be corrected to read EAS before applying the appropriate construction. Having thus obtained the best speeds to fly for various thermal strengths, for example, these are then corrected back to IAS for use by the pilot.

Other Errors

Errors in the static pressure will affect not only the airspeed indicator but also, in principle, the altimeter. However, for sailplanes, these errors are normally negligible. There is also Compressibility Error, which afflicts rather faster aircraft because the relationship between the pressure difference across the ASI and the indicated airspeed depends not only on the latter but also on the Mach number, and there can be an interaction between the Pressure and Compressibilty errors as well. Fortunately, we do not need to concern ourselves with such matters.

Finally, there is a source of much misunderstanding: the reduction of V_{NE} with height to avoid flutter. JAR-22 is somewhat coy about flutter and at present it is best to consult OSTIVAS, which states that sailplanes must be free from aeroelastic effects up to V_{DF} at heights up to 3000 m and at selected speeds up to V_{DF} at greater altitudes. A footnote in the latter case states that speeds equivalent to the True Airspeed corresponding to V_{DF} at 3000 m are normally found to be safe. Compliance must be demonstrated by flight flutter tests as close as is practicable to 3000 m and not less than 2000 m. The damping must be adequate and must not decrease rapidly as V_{DF} is approached. In addition, analytically determined flutter speeds must not be less than 1.2 V_{DF} at altitudes up to 3000 m and 1.2 times the "selected speeds" at greater altitudes. In practice, most machines have a constant IAS limitation up to 3000 m (or 10,000 ft) and a limitation corresponding to a constant TAS at greater heights, leading to a marked reduction in IAS.

The point of this situation is that there is no way of discussing flutter in simple physical terms, because it almost certainly involves controls in modern sailplanes. (See, for example, Chajec (1993).) Putting it rather crudely, if we consider a wing and aileron, the aileron being unbalanced, in that its centre of mass is behind the pivot point, then when the wing is accelerating downwards it will tend to leave the aileron behind and this will produce an aerodynamic force tending to reinforce the motion. In practice, the situation is obviously more complicated than this very simplified picture would suggest and the analysis becomes quite difficult. There have been cases in which a preliminary calculation suggests that the flutter speed will be even less than the constant TAS rule would suggest, but a certain amount of mass balance, thus moving the centre of mass of the controls forward, has so far sufficed to get the flutter speed to more than 1.2 times the TAS limit.

To summarize, a constant TAS rule at altitudes above 3000 m is not a law of nature but it simply gives a rule which, so far, has been very satisfactory. The corollary is that it is vital to ensure that mass balance weights are always properly attached.

References

Joint Airworthiness Requirements: JAR-22, Sailplanes and Powered Sailplanes. Printed and distributed by the Civil Aviation Authority, Printing and Publications Services, Greville House, 37, Gratton Road, Cheltenham, Glos. GL50 2BN, England, on behalf of the Airworthiness Authorities Steering Committee.

OSTIV Airworthiness Standards for Sailplanes, March '96. Published by the Organisation Scientifique et Technique Internationale du Vol a Voile, c/o Tu-Delft, Fac. Aerospace Engin. Kluyerweg 1. NL-2629 HS Delft, the Netherlands.

Chajec, W.C., "Critical flutter speed of sailplanes calculated for high altitude", *Technical Soaring*, **18**(3) 1994.

SECTION C:
THE SAILPLANE IN THE ATMOSPHERE

Chapter 7

THE SAILPLANE IN THE ATMOSPHERE

Sailplanes rely on motions of the atmosphere to achieve sustained flight and the object of this chapter is to consider some of these motions. Thermals were known to the Wright Brothers in 1901, but were first really discovered in 1921 by one William Leusch at the Wasserkuppe. Professor Georgii was eventually to start a programme in 1928 to investigate the lift under cumulus clouds. Such lift was first exploited by Kronfeld at the same time and within a year he had achieved a distance of 85.5 miles, flying his new sailplane, the "Wien". By 1930, he had taken a variometer with him and was able to locate the invisible rising air: for him, and many another pilot, the way was open to exploit it. The first genuine thermal soaring, without the help of hills or thunderstorms, took place in the United States under the auspices of an American pilot, A. Haller, and Wolf Hirth. So thermal soaring is only 68 years old.

Thermals in the Laboratory

Many experiments were carried out in the then Department of Meteorology, Imperial College, in the 1950s (e.g., Scorer (1956) and Woodward (1956)) which served to explain many of the prevailing beliefs about thermals. In Scorer's experiments, the "thermals" consisted of bubbles of salt solution released near the top of ordinary water in a suitable chamber. The salt ensured that the density of the "thermal" exceeded that of the fresh water, and it was rendered visible by inserting a white precipitate. The density of the surrounding water was uniform, corresponding to an adiabatic lapse rate in the real atmosphere. The

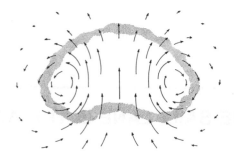

Fig. 7.1. A "vortex ring" thermal. The lengths of the bubbles indicate the local air velocities.

actual density of the salt solution was of little consequence: all that happened was that the greater the density difference, the greater were all the velocities. Motions behind the bubble were small and the trailing material was very tenuous. The general motion was very like that of a vortex ring and the most interesting feature of such a flow is that the vertical velocity in the centre is greater than the rate of rise of the thermal. (See Fig. 7.1). As long as this difference in velocity exceeds the sinking speed of the sailplane, it will rise in relation to the thermal. It will continue to rise until the difference in vertical velocities is equal to the rate of sink and will then continue upwards at the rate of rise of the bubble as a whole. A consequence is that sailplanes of greatly different performances will eventually all climb at the same rate — the rate of ascent of the bubble as a whole — but with higher performance machines towards the top of the stack.

Betsy Woodward expanded this picture by considering the velocities, both vertical and horizontal, within such a thermal. She also took into account an effect proposed by Goodhart (1956), to the effect that circling in an outflow is to increase the rate of sink, and in an inflow to decrease it. This analysis further confirmed various observations made by pilots.

It is worth noting that these "thermals" represent but one type, and indeed Betsy remarks that "It is felt that a thermal leaving the ground is generally in the form of a "column", i.e., after a short time its vertical dimensions are greater than its horizontal.... Eventually the column becomes detached from the ground and we may call it a "sausage".

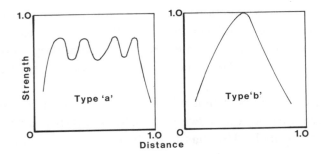

Fig. 7.2. Thermal profiles according to Konovalov. The slight asymmetry may be due to the instrumentation.

Because mixing with the surrounding air takes place primarily at the top of the "sausage", the tail will rise in relation to the top and eventually we will have an isolated thermal. In these experiments, we are looking at thermals in a substantially neutral atmosphere, and it would be surprising if there was not a considerable variety of thermal types associated with other types of atmosphere.

Thermals in Practice

Simultaneously, many experiments were carried out to try to determine what thermals were really like, particularly from the point of view of the sailplane pilot. Perhaps the best set of results was obtained by the Russian meteorologist D.A. Konovalov (1970), based on 377 traverses of thermals in Estonia carried out by a Blanik sailplane and a Yak-12 light aeroplane. Two basic types of thermals were identified: type "a" containing several maxima with depressions in between and type "b" with one pronounced maximum. (See Fig. 7.2.) The cross-section of type "b" is almost exactly triangular whilst that of type "a" shows a much wider region of strong lift. An attempt was made to relate the type of thermal with the vertical gradient of temperature in the lower 300 m of the atmosphere, from which it seems that if the gradient is roughly −0.8°/100 m, both types occur with the same frequency. At lower values of the gradient, type "b" is the more common and at higher values type "a" is prevalent, leading to the supposition that type "b" represents the original element of convection, several of which converge to form type "a" when convective conditions improve. Whilst these results convey a good air of verisimilitude, we must remember that they were all taken in a small area of the Baltic state, and may not be representative of elsewhere.

We would also expect that what goes up in one place must come down somewhere else, and hence we would expect to find downdraughts between the thermals. This has been investigated by Johnson (1978), who concluded that in Texas the average apparent inter-thermal downdraft strength is roughly one-tenth of the gross thermal strength and that the average thermal height is roughly one-tenth of the thermal spacing. There was, of course, considerable scatter in these results. These results show that a sailplane with an effective inter-thermal glide ratio of 20 or better has a high probability of reaching the next thermal at a sufficient height to climb away. A glide ratio of 10 provides a probability of less than 0.5 that the next thermal will be reached. Johnson remarks that "... the modern sailplane's 40 to 1 capability provides their pilots little excuse for landing prematurely under normal convective conditions".

Mathematical Descriptions

These are required for two purposes: to facilitate handicapping and to provide a picture which corresponds reasonably closely to reality, thus enabling designers to "fly" their concepts under something like the conditions which actually prevail. There is no need for both sets of conditions to apply simultaneously, and indeed they frequently do not. It is obvious that whatever model is chosen it should have a smooth gradation of velocity with distance from the axis since, in a real atmosphere, turbulence and viscosity will tend to prevent the occurrence of sharp steps in both the velocity and velocity gradient. A more elaborate requirement is that the velocity distribution should be such that the principle of continuity is satisfied (i.e., there should be regions of down-draught associated with the up-current, so that there is no net transport of the atmosphere into outer space or through the Earth). The vertical velocity will then taper off to zero at large distances from the axis, but if we are only interested in conditions fairly close to the core, this requirement need not necessarily be simulated.

Power-Law Velocity Distributions

These are purely mathematical idealisations, with no physical justification except that they satisfy the first of the above requirements, close to the axis and can provide realistic results if the numbers are appropriately chosen. They assume an expression of the following type:

$$V_T/V_{To} = 1 - (r/R)^n \qquad (7.1)$$

where V_{To} is the vertical velocity on the axis, where $r = 1$, and R is the "thermal radius", i.e., the value of r at which $V_T = 0$. The index n is conveniently taken to be an integer. If $n = 1$, the thermal is triangular, and it therefore has a discontinuity in velocity at $r = 0$ which, for reasons explained above, is unlikely to be realistic. However, such a thermal is not too unlike Konovalov "a", which can therefore be regarded as having an index n slightly greater than 1.0. Putting $n = 2$ gives a parabolic profile, as commonly adopted for simple analyses. For example, the thermal used for BGA handicapping purposes has $n = 2$, $V_{To} = 4.2$ knots and $R = 1000$ ft. It therefore corresponds to:

$$V_T = 4.2\left[1 - (r/1000)^2\right]. \qquad (7.2)$$

Other Parabolic Thermals

In Germany a more general expression has been adopted (Quast, 1965):

$$V_T = ar^2 + br + c \qquad (7.3)$$

which, by a suitable choice of the parameters a, b and c, can be used to describe a strong or a weak thermal, or a wide thermal. The strong thermal has a core strength of about 6.2 m/s whilst the weak one is about half this strength. Both have a radius, where the up-draught velocity is zero, of about 120 m. The wide thermal has a core strength of about 4.6 m/s and a radius of about 160 m. These thermals are principally used in determining the performance of a given sailplane in various thermals, whereas the British device gives a single figure of merit for handicapping purposes.

Spherical Bubbles

One concept of a thermal, as we have seen, corresponds to a bubble ascending through the atmosphere. If we asume the bubble to be spherical with no mixing at its surface, then the vertical velocity profile will be given by;

$$V_T/V_{T_0} = \left[1 - (r/R)^2\right] / \left[1 + 2(r/R)^2\right]^{5/2}. \qquad (7.4)$$

This may look fairly plausible, but leads to a large region of low vertical velocity towards the outer regions. The velocity gradient up to about $r/R = 0.5$ is fairly close to parabolic and the above expression corresponds to a "doublet" located at the centre of the sphere. The above expression only defines the shape of the vertical velocity distribution and is independent of height relative to the centre of the bubble. Strictly, it does not apply in the equatorial plane of the bubble, since the doublet causes the vertical velocity to become infinite at the centre. Also, R is not the radius of the bubble at the section under consideration, nor is V_{T_0} the rate of ascent of the bubble as a whole. Further information may be found in Batchelor, 1967, Chapter 7.

Another type of spherical bubble is "Hill's spherical vortex". This was adopted by Larrabee, 1974, to consider the behaviour of a sailplane in a thermal, and is somewhat akin to the vortex ring concept, except that the vorticity is distributed over the whole interior of the spherical bubble according to a particular law. In the simpler bubble considered above, all the vorticity is concentrated at its centre. The vertical velocity distribution within the bubble is parabolic, again lending some credence to this simple distribution, and that outside will be the same as for the previous spherical bubble, with the tangential velocities inside and outside matching at the surface. This leads to a discontinuity in velocity gradient at the surface. Larrabee was of the opinion that its vertical velocity distribution matched quite closely that observed by Woodward. Again, see Batchelor for more details. Both of these types of spherical bubbles satisfy the principle of continuity.

A Modified Parabolic Distribution

A velocity distribution proposed by Gedeon (1972), for the purpose of analysing "dolphin" flying was of the form

$$V_T / V_{To} = \left[1 - \left(r/R \right)^2 \right] \exp \left[- \left(r/R \right)^2 \right] . \tag{7.5}$$

This gives an expression rather similar to the spherical bubble and satisfies the continuity requirement. It has no basis in theory or in experiment but is simply a plausible-looking mathematical expression. However, it is useful in the analysis of cloud street flying, since once continuity is satisfied, any number of such thermals of assorted strength may be strung together with arbitrary distances between the cores.

General Remarks on Thermals

The above remarks on the theoretical shapes of thermals are all very well and the BGA handicapping system seems to work quite satisfactorily: at all events, there seem to be no severe complaints about it. But it does leave some fundamental questions unanswered. Why, in particular, have so few measurements been made of real thermals? The trouble is that the structure of thermals is mainly of interest to the glider pilot; to other pilots, they are simply turbulence. The measurements we require are extremely difficult to make, due to the variability and invisibility of thermals, instrumentation, and the organisation required. The mind boggles at the organisation required for Konovalov's 377 traverses of thermals. For example, Milford (1972), tried flying through thermals in an instrumented two-seat sailplane and found that few of them showed the sorts of structure assumed above. However, it is worth saying that the vertical response of the sailplane was not particularly well organised by current standards and the thermals were mostly rather weak. However, it was found that the temperature excesses were typically 0.5°C at 300 m above the ground, falling off with height until they could be zero at 1000 m, even in good British conditions. The bouyancy appears to be then due to changes in humidity.

Cloud Streets

These, together with many other interesting features of thermals, are discussed by Scorer (1978). Cloud streets consist of cumulus arranged in fairly straight lines roughly along the wind and are usually spaced at about twice the cloud base height apart. They are the glider pilot's dream, provided the desired track is not too far from their direction, and satellite pictures show cloud streets encompassing whole countries. However, they are rather rare, and the more usual observation is that the thermals are arranged in a rather random fashion. There are occasions when thermals are "blue", i.e., the condensation level is above the top of the convection, and then the sailplane pilot can fly for considerable distances without encountering any lift. He is flying between the rows of thermals, which are invisible, but a small deviation to either side will put him in rising air.

Waves

Waves are large-scale disturbances produced by ground features when a wind is blowing past them. Their effects were known long before the nature of the flow was understood and many have local names, such as the Helm Wind. The phenomenon is treated extensively in Scorer (1978).

Waves were originally thought to be rather rare, but are now known to be fairly common, to the extent that the author and many other pilots have soared in a wave, in the vicinity of Lasham, where no significant upwind feature was visible. If conditions are suitable and steady, the wave system will remain fixed relative to the ground feature which produces it and it may extend to many times the height of the feature. The conditions favourable for wave formation are extremely various and when coupled with the wide variety of ground features, an almost infinite variety of waves exists. When the conditions are not steady, the geometry of the wave pattern will change accordingly. In two dimensions,

Scorer has shown that, for a single obstacle of a given height, the amplitude of lee waves is a maximum when the half-width of the obstacle is about $1/\pi$ times the wavelength. It is commonly found that the up-going part of a wave is uncannily smooth, whilst the down-going part is often extremely turbulent.

In three dimensions, the picture is even more complicated. A single conical mountain will often produce a pattern like that due to a boat moving through water. If mountains are arranged in series, the patterns may tend to reinforce one another, or to cancel out. West (1996), has published some results showing the interference patterns due to ridges at various alignments, some of which are very complicated. Further remarks on flying in waves are to be found in Chapter 11.

The Wind

The wind obviously affects the behaviour of sailplanes in respect to how the pilot deals with cross-wind flights in the presence of cloud streets, the final glide, wave-flying and ordinary hill-flying. Also, it is important to remember the wind gradient and gustiness when landing. Some of these topics will be considered in the appropriate places, but it is worth mentioning the investigation of Crawley and Schmanske (1993), who considered the flow over two models of ridges in the Wright Brothers' wind tunnel at MIT, which included variations in incoming flow angle, ground roughness and the earth's boundary layer. Previous investigations had been confined to simple potential flows at right angles to two-dimensional ridges represented in some simple fashion. For example, if the ridge is semi-circular, the line of optimum lift is at $45°$, extending forwards from the ridge. This is no longer true under more realistic conditions, and the reader is referred to the original paper for a discussion of all the conditions tested.

The Standard Atmosphere

To provide an agreed basis for the calibration of aircraft instruments and for carrying out performance calculations, it is necessary to define a standard atmosphere. This may not have much relation to a real atmosphere in which soaring can be conducted, but it is important to know that it exists. A number of such standards have been derived from 1920s onwards: those in current use are the US Standard Atmosphere, 1976, the ISO Standard Atmosphere, 1973 and the ICAO Standard Atmosphere, 1964. They are identical up to a height of 32 km.

The Standard Atmosphere is intended to represent the long-term average properties of the atmosphere at a latitude of 45°. It incorporates certain idealisations: for example, the air is assumed to be a dry perfect gas. Taking accepted standard sea-level values of sea-level pressure and temperature, and assuming a suitable lapse rate, rounded off to a convenient value, the properties of the atmosphere can be derived as functions of height, as tabulated in the Appendix.

In a uniform gravitational field, the computations involved in defining a Standard Atmosphere would be quite simple. However, the acceleration due to gravity is a function of height and latitude. The simplest assumptions (a spherically symmetrical non-rotating Earth) would suggest that g varies inversely as the square of the distance from the Earth's centre. In practice, rotation of the Earth and a departure from spherical symmetry render the relationship more complicated. For the purpose of defining a Standard Atmosphere, the independent variable loosely termed "height" above is the "geopotential altitude".

If the geopotential altitude is Z then the geopotential altitude is h, where

$$h = \int (g/g_o)dZ \tag{7.6}$$

and the integral is taken from 0 to Z. In this expression, g is a function of Z at 45° and g_o corresponds to $Z = 0$. The geopotential altitude is therefore an equivalent altitude in a constant gravitational field g_o: a body, or a particle of air, at (h, g_o) has the same potential energy as it would have had at (Z, g). For the purpose of aircraft performance calculations, it is also convenient to work in terms of geopotential altitude since the aircraft itself can be regarded as operating in a constant gravitational field.

Tabulated data are expressed in terms of geopotential altitude as the independent variable and were originally calculated in metric units.

The tabulated data in English units are derived by use of the usual conversion factors. As one would expect, there is little difference between h and Z in the lower atmosphere. At the tropopause, $h = 11000$ m and $Z = 11019$ m.

On a given day, the actual atmosphere differs from standard. When the performance of a sailplane is measured under non-standard conditions, it is necessary to correct the performance to standard conditions, for which purpose the departures of the atmosphere from standard must be known, e.g. from radio-sonde ascents. It is particularly important to do so if the performance is measured on different days with different conditions and if one is measuring the performance of a powered sailplane with little excess of power, it will be even more important to do so.

Since an altimeter is basically a pressure-measuring instrument calibrated in accordance with the Standard Atmosphere, the pilot normally deals with "pressure height" (i.e., the geopotential altitude which, in the Standard Atmosphere, would correspond with the local air pressure at the sailplane's actual location). In effect, this is the reading of a perfect altimeter, free from errors due to its installation in the sailplane. Official height records are conventionally pressure heights.

References

Batchelor, G.K., *An Introduction to Fluid Dynamics*, Cambridge, 1967, pp. 521–526.

Gedeon, J., "Dynamic analysis of dolphin-style thermal cross-country flight", *OSTIV Publication* **XII**, 1972.

Goodhart, H.C.N., "Circling flight in a radial field of flow", *OSTIV Publication* **IV**, 1956.

Johnson, R.H., "Measurements of sailplane sink rates between thermals", *OSTIV Publication* **XV**, 1978.

Konovalov, D.A., "On the structure of thermals", *OSTIV Publication* **XI**, 1970.

Larrabee, E.E. "Lateral control and sailplane design considerations to optimize altitude gain whilst thermalling", *Proceedings of the Second International Symposium on the Technology and Science of Low-speed and Motorless Flight.* Massachusetts Institute of Technology, 1974.

Milford, J.R., "Some thermal sections shown by an instrumented glider", *OSTIV Publication* **XII**, 1972.

Quast, A., "Computer calculations on optimum rate of climb in parabolic thermals", *OSTIV Publication* **IX** (Part II), 1965.

Scorer, R.S., "Experiments with convection bubbles", *OSTIV Publication* **IV**, 1956.

Scorer, R.S., *Environmental Aerodynamics*, Ellis Horwood, Chichester (John Wiley & Sons), 1978, pp. 340–343 and 191–194.

West, J., "Lee wave interference patterns", *Technical Soaring*, April, 1996.

Woodward, B., "A theory of thermal soaring", *OSTIV Publication* **IV**, 1956.

Chapter 8

FLYING IN THERMALS:
THE CLASSICAL ANALYSIS

The Optimum Rate of Climb

In Chapter 4, the equations of motion of a sailplane were obtained and in Fig. 4.5 plots of rate of sink for various angles of bank were deduced. It is then a simple matter to find the condition at which the rate of sink is a minimum: for each angle of bank there will be a speed at which the rate of sink will be a minimum. Incidentally, in this analysis, all speeds are "equivalent" unless stated otherwise. This leads to the upper curve of Fig. 4.5. (The lower curve corresponds to a different wing loading).

We now take a curve of rate of ascent of the air against radius for whatever thermal we wish to consider. In this case, we will look at the "British Standard Thermal", corresponding to Eq. (7.2). This curve is plotted in Fig. 8.1, and subtracted from it is the rate of sink at $w = 6.7$ lb/ft^2, so that the lower curve corresponds to the rate of climb at various angles of bank and the best speed. It will be seen that the optimum angle of bank is about 35°, the corresponding speed is about 49 knots and the best rate of climb is 2.3 knots. Here, it is assumed that the pilot is flying perfectly within this rather artificial framework.

In fact, we do not need to do all this tedious curve-plotting for the parabolic thermal. The optimum circling performance of a sailplane is entirely determined by the minimum rate of sink $V_{s\,min}$ and the corresponding forward speed V_{ms} in straight flight. The optimum angle of bank ϕ is then that which satisfies

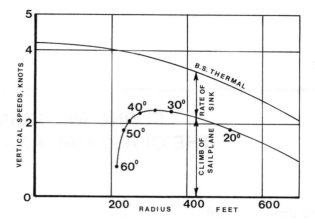

Fig. 8.1. The maximum rate of climb in a "British Standard Thermal". The optimum angle of bank is about 35° and the rate of climb is about 2.4 knots.

$$3\tan^4\phi\,\cos^{\frac{1}{2}}\phi = 4\left(V_{ms}^2/gR\right)^2\left(V_{To}/V_{Smin}\right). \qquad (8.1)$$

The value of ϕ so obtained is then inserted in the following equation to obtain the maximum rate of climb:

$$V_c/V_{smin} = \left(V_{To}/V_{smin}\right)\left[1 - \left(V_{ms}^2/gR\right)^2\cosec^2\phi\right] - \left(\sec\phi\right)^{\frac{3}{2}}. \qquad (8.2)$$

It is therefore possible to calculate the maximum rate of climb of any glider in a parabolic thermal. We will see what use we can make of this analysis later.

A Little History

For some time before the war, pilots were aware that one should fly faster in down-currents so as to traverse them quickly. Indeed, the construction to obtain the best gliding angle under such circumstances was well known. But what about the speed to fly so as to make the average speed as high as possible? In 1938, one Wolfgang Spate used tables developed during the previous year giving the best speeds between thermals, but neglecting down-currents. In the same year two Poles,

L. Swarz and W. Kasprzyk, also published their results which now included the effect of air mass movement between the thermals. The Spate result was published in the UK by Philip Wills in 1940, using the pen-name "Corunus". This was more or less forgotten in the press of war and the next efforts were in the form of two letters published quite independently in the same copy of "Sailplane and Glider", in June 1947. The authors were G.W. Pirie and E. Dewing, members of the Cambridge University Gliding Club. Pirie derived his result by physical argument, but Dewing waded straight into the mathematics and obtained the results quoted below.

His letter ends a little forlornly: "It is realised that the whole business is getting too complicated and this is only an ideal to be aimed at; but it should give a reasonable indication of the speed and direction most likely to give the best results". However, all was to change a couple of years later when Paul MacCready published a paper in the November 1949 issue of Schweizer Aero Review, to be followed by a correction by Dr Karl Nickel in December, pointing out a minor confusion in the mathematics. The American version did not appear until the March/April 1954 edition of "Soaring" when Paul MacCready published his paper on the "Optimum Airspeed Selector", presumably with slight corrections, since the formula attributed to him by Dr Nickel does not explicitly appear. This explained the now-familiar MacCready ring (see Chapter 9) and not just the version applied to linear variometers: he suggested a variant with different scales for various thermal strengths for use with non-linear instruments. So, whilst MacCready did us a great service in proposing his ring, the basic theory was around long before him. It would only be fair to refer to the theory as "The Classical Theory", and reserve mention of MacCready to the ring setting and an analogous process in electric variometer devices.

It is noteworthy that, in Dewing's letter and in Reichman's book (1978) the sequence is glide-climb instead of climb-glide. The argument, it is supposed, is that when you have finished a climb, it is behind you, so how can it affect the following glide? But it can equally be argued that when you have finished a glide, it is equally behind you so how can it affect the next climb? The fact of the matter is that the

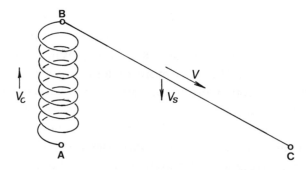

Fig. 8.2. An idealised section of a cross-country flight.

sequence does not matter at this elementary level, but putting the climb first seems more natural: you know what the average rate of climb was, and you can then control the glide accordingly, whereas with the opposite sequence the pilot is already being required to exercise powers of prophecy.

The Classical Analysis

The theory which follows can be regarded as the Classical Analysis, even if it differs in some minor features from the original. It has its limitations, some of them quite severe, but it is the basis of all subsequent optimisations and therefore needs to be considered rather closely.

The object of the analysis is to maximise the cross-country speed. This is obviously required for breaking speed records but it is also true for any distance flight, where the flight is often limited by the useful length of the day. We will initially consider only one climb-glide sequence, as shown in Fig. 8.2. The sailplane is assumed to climb from A to B with an average rate of climb V_c. Although we have seen how to maximise the rate of climb in the first paragraph of this chapter, we do not need to do so here: all we need to know is the average climb rate actually achieved in the thermal. Any gain in height at A, as one slows down from the previous glide, or loss at B, as one speeds up for the next glide, are taken into account in reckoning V_c. At B, the sailplane stops turning and flies straight to C at speed V and rate of sink V_s. Also,

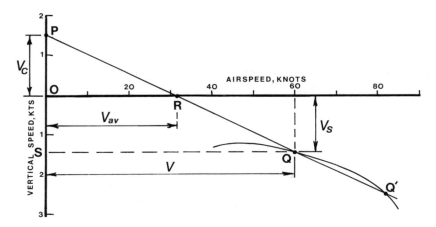

Fig. 8.3. Construction to show the average speed attained.

C is taken to be at the same height as A and for the moment up- or down-currents between B and C are neglected. Also, both A and B are close to sea-level, so that the difference between true and equivalent speeds is negligible. This is, indeed, a very formalised element of a cross-country flight.

If the time spent climbing is t_c then the height gained will be $V_c\, t_c$. If the pilot glides from B to C in time t_g then the loss of height will be $t_g\, V_s$. Equating the gain and loss of height, it follows that

$$t_g = V_c\, t_c / V_s \tag{8.3}$$

and hence the distance covered is

$$t_g V = V_c\, t_c V / V_s . \tag{8.4}$$

The total time for the climb and glide will be

$$t_c + t_g = t_c \left(1 + V_c / V_s \right) . \tag{8.5}$$

So, dividing the total distance by the total time, the average speed is:

$$V_{av} = V\; V_c / \left(V_s + V_c \right) \tag{8.6}$$

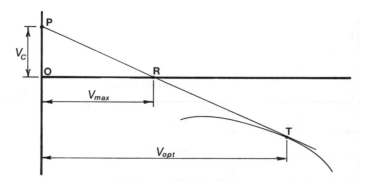

Fig. 8.4. Construction to show the maximum speed attained.

and the problem is then to choose V so as to make V_{av} a maximum, V_c being known.

Consider the construction shown in Fig. 8.3 superimposed on the polar diagram of the sailplane. From a point P, such that OP represents V_c to a suitable scale, a line is drawn to a point Q on the polar. Q represents the conditions V and V_s during the glide. Triangles POR and PSQ are similar and hence the relationship between the various speeds corresponds to Eq. (8.6), if V_{av} is represented by OR. By a similar argument, the same average speed is obtained by flying at conditions corresponding to the point Q'.

It is immediately apparent that V_{av} is maximised by arranging for PR produced to be tangential to the polar, as in Fig. 8.4. The point T then represents the optimum speed to glide, V_{opt}, and OR represents V_{max}, the maximum average speed. It is clear that any other gliding speed, represented by Q or Q', gives a lower average speed.

The condition corresponding to Fig. 8.4 is that, at the optimum gliding speed, the slope of the polar must have the value PS/PT or, in the symbols of the calculus, at $V = V_{opt}$:

$$dV_s/dV = (V_s + V_c)/V, \qquad (8.7)$$

a result which could also have been obtained by differentiating Eq. (8.6). It will be seen in Chapter 11 that this is but one example of a more general construction.

It is implicit in the above that either the horizontal distance AC or the height gained AB is fixed. In the former case the analysis tells us how to cover the distance AC as rapidly as possible. Once the rate of climb V_c is known, then the optimum gliding speed V_{opt} is also known and hence the gliding angle, V_s/V_{opt}. Then the height to be gained will be the distance AC multiplied by the gliding angle.

Conversely, if the height AB is fixed, in a similar manner we can calculate the horizontal distance AC. With a rate of climb V_c, the analysis now tells us how to cover the distance AC as rapidly as possible, although AC is now determined by the height of the climb and the rate of climb.

In practice, these considerations are seldom of much consequence. Consider the idealised case of a cross-country flight in which all the thermals are of the same strength but at different distances apart, but never so far that we cannot fly at V_{opt} whenever glides occur. (The sailplane can always be flown at some lower speed to obtain a better glide angle, at the expense of a lower average speed.) In any one glide, the final height will generally be different from the initial height. If we simply consider a single glide of this nature, as when taking off from a hill site and landing in the valley below, then an analysis similar to the above will show that the optimum speed is no longer V_{opt}. However, if in the course of a substantial flight, we add together all of the climbs and all of the glides, we get back to something very close to the original construction. The difference will be that the initial and final heights will differ by the launch height, plus any difference if the flight does not end where it began. This effect will generally be negligible, except in the case of a short flight, say 100 km, performed by a very high-performance sailplane. Also, the only moment at which we need to consider the horizontal distance will be to decide how high we need to climb in the last thermal, for which see Chapter 9.

Effect of Down-Currents

We have already seen that there will be down-currents between the thermals, and these must obviously be taken into account in constructions for the best gliding speed. It really amounts to supposing that, temporarily, we have a worse sailplane, the sinking speed being increased by the

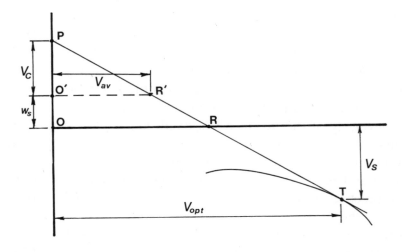

Fig. 8.5. Construction to show the maximum speed attained in the presence of a down-current.

downdraught velocity. Therefore, we simply move the origin from O to O', as in Fig. 8.5, where OO' corresponds to w_s, the downwards air velocity. The instantaneous value of V_{av} is now

$$V_{av} = VV_c/(V_s + V_c + w_s) \tag{8.8}$$

and the criterion for maximising this quantity is that at $V = V_{opt}$,

$$dV_s/dV = (V_s + V_c + w_s)/V. \tag{8.9}$$

It may seem a little curious that whereas V_c is the average rate of climb for the whole thermal, w_s is a quantity which changes from one moment to the next. I cannot think of a better way of explaining this than to use Karl Nickel's words: "Imagine the part of the flight between the thermals to be divided into as many parts as there are different values of [w_s], and that associated with each part is an amount of thermal climb necessary to regain the height lost in that part. Then the [formula 8.9] is valid for each part and so the best speed to fly in that part can be obtained by the usual construction. Hence the method ... remains valid even when the sink varies along the flight path".

Whilst Eq. (8.8) tells us the instantaneous average speed, it will not tell us the average speed for the whole climb-glide sequence. The expression is quite complicated, involving integrals, and is not of much interest in practice. Also, the speed V is now varying, and hence so will be the total variometer reading, thus rendering a total energy variometer quite essential. In fact, one must go for a better device than this, for as w_s changes and the pilot tries to adjust his speed accordingly, the rate of sink of the sailplane, V_s, also changes. So, if the pilot is using the normal MacCready ring (see Chapter 9), he will be chasing the variometer, even if it is of the total energy type. However, as explained in Chapter 9, this effect can be removed from the variometer readings.

The BGA Handicapping System

At the beginning of this chapter, we saw how to calculate the maximum rate of climb attainable in a parabolic thermal. The basis of the BGA handicapping system is now clear: we obtain the maximum rate of climb of a given sailplane in the BGA standard thermal (4.2 knots maximum, with a radius of 1,000 ft) and then use this in conjunction with a construction as in Fig. 8.4 to obtain the average cross-country speed. This is then compared with the speed of a sailplane handicapped at 100 (ASW-15, DG-100, Hornet, LS-1, SHK-1, Std. Cirrus) to get the final figure. Thus the ASW-24 will have a rate of climb of 2.4 knots, giving an average speed of 38.5 knots, and a handicap figure of 105. In practice, this system is not followed exactly and the Handicap Sub-committee has introduced some variations. (See Spencer, (1993)).

References

Dewing, E., Letter to *Sailplane and Glider*, June 1947.

MacCready, P.B., "Optimum airspeed selector", *Soaring*, March–April, 1954.

Nickel, K.L.E., "The best speed for cross-country soaring", *Swiss Aero-Revue*, December, 1949. Reprinted with some editing by A.F.W. Edwards, *Sailplane and Gliding*, December 1994–January 1995.

Pirie, G.W., Letter to *Sailplane and Glider*, June 1947.

Spencer, J., "The new BGA handicap list", *Sailplane and Gliding Yearbook*, 1993.

I am indebted to Dr A.F.W. Edwards of the Cambridge Gliding Club for some of the historical information at the beginning of this Chapter.

Chapter 9

SOME IDEAS ON THE PRACTICE OF
CROSS-COUNTRY FLYING

It would be nice if the pilot could be provided with some simple indication of the best speed to fly, in accordance with Eq. (8.9), from the information readily available in the cockpit. First, consider the results of finding the best speed to fly for various thermal strengths, assuming that the air between the thermals is stationary. In effect we draw tangents from various values of V_c to the polar curve, as indicated by Eq. (8.7). The results for the ASW-24 at a wing loading of 6.7 lb/ft^2 are as follows:

Table 9.1.

V_c knots	V knots between thermals	V_{av} knots average speed
0.20	55	7.42
0.71	60	19.84
1.28	65	28.50
1.92	70	35.29
2.64	75	41.01
3.44	80	46.08
4.34	85	50.70
5.34	90	55.03

It is now clear that the values displayed in the first column of this table are also applicable to the situation displayed in Fig. 8.5 provided that they now represent $V_c + w_s$. The table may now be modified by adding to the figures in the first column, the still-air rates of sink V_s corresponding to the values of V in the second column, thus giving $(V_s + V_c + w_s)$ as in Table 9.2. Figures for V_{av} are now omitted since they are no longer very relevant. Also, since w_s has been treated as a downdraught for the purposes of this analysis, it can have either sign in practice. In the present convention, a positive sign represents a downdraught and a negative sign an updraught.

Table 9.2.

V knots between thermals	V_s knots	$V_s + V_c + w_s$ knots
55	1.28	1.48
60	1.44	2.15
65	1.64	2.92
70	1.89	3.81
75	2.19	4.83
80	2.54	5.98
85	2.94	7.28
90	3.39	8.73

In Table 9.2, values of V_s are given for the various values of V, to aid this calculation.

Now consider the device shown in Fig. 9.1. A rotatable ring surrounds the variometer and, with the datum mark set to zero, speeds corresponding to the first column above are marked opposite sink indications on the variometer scale corresponding to the third column. For example, 70 knots is opposite to a sink value of 3.81 knots on the variometer scale.

For use in flight, the ring is rotated so that its datum is opposite the figure on the rate of climb scale corresponding to the pilot's estimate of V_c. When flying between thermals, the variometer will show a sink reading of $V_s + w_s$, and hence, the speed to fly will be the figure on the ring opposite this value. For example, if the rate of climb is 2.5 knots

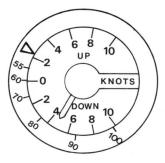

Fig. 9.1. The MacCready ring.

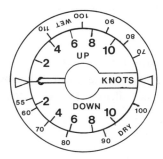

Fig. 9.2. The MacCready ring modified to deal with two weights of the sailplane.

and the variometer shows a rate of sink of 4.7 knots, then the speed to fly is 84 knots. This is the MacCready ring, whose use has become nearly universal. In this form, it can only be used with a linear-scale variometer, such as the Winter or PZL, but this is not now a significant limitation. Originally, Paul MacCready also proposed a system for variometers with non-linear scales, but this was a clumsy system involving a series of interchangeable rings. Strictly, a separate ring is required for each different weight of the sailplane, but in practice, it suffices to have two scales: one for normal maximum weight and the other for the maximum weight with water. Both scales can easily be incorporated into the same ring, as in Fig. 9.2.

Working out the markings on the MacCready ring by literally drawing tangents to the polar is, in practice, highly unsatisfactory. It is remarkably

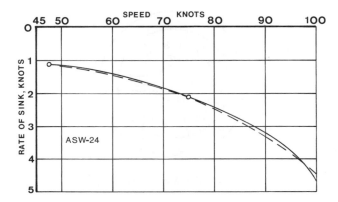

Fig. 9.3. The polar of the ASW-24 with an approximate analytical curve, shown dotted.

difficult to draw proper tangents and the speed figures are then scattered around the ring in an unconvicing fashion. It is normally better to proceed in an analytical fashion, as follows. Equation (4.12) for the rate of sink was:

$$2V_{si}/V_{sio} = \left(V_i/V_{io}\right)^3 + \left(V_{io}/V_i\right). \tag{9.1}$$

We now wish to transfer a curve having this form to an actual polar, as nearly as possible. In general, such a curve can only be made to pass through two measured points, by taking two sets of values of V and V_s (or V_i and V_{si}) and substituting in the above equation to give two simultaneous equations in V_{io} and V_{sio} (or V_0 and V_{so}). Figure 9.3 shows that the agreement can be very good indeed if the two points are chosen prudently. On the one hand, they should not be too close together, but on the other, they should not be too close to the low-speed and very high-speed ends of the curve. The optimum speed between thermals for a given rate of climb is then given by solving

$$V_c/V_{so} = \left(V/V_o\right)^3 - \left(V_o/V\right), \tag{9.2}$$

as can easily be shown by differentiating the previous equation. Also, the quantity $V_s + V_c + w_s$ can be obtained by adding Eqs. (9.1) and (9.2), remembering that $V_c + w_s$ can replace V_c. Hence we get:

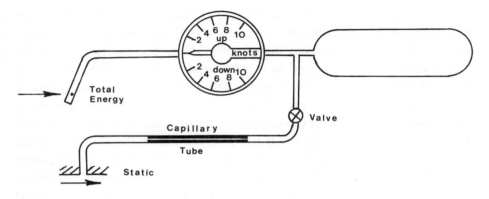

Fig. 9.4. The variometer arranged to show air mass movement.

$$(V_s + V_c + w_s) = \tfrac{1}{2}\left[3(V/V_o)^3 - V_o/V\right] \qquad (9.3)$$

Hence, choosing a suitable series of values of V, we can find $V_s + V_c + w_s$ and hence complete the table, as in Table 9.2. This all lends itself to devising a simple computation programme and in fact Table 9.2 was obtained in just this fashion.

Little Tricks with Variometers

Chapter 5 indicated that the variometer could be induced to display Air Mass Movements. The point of doing so is that even with total energy, there is still an element of successive approximation in interpreting variometer readings in the gliding mode. Suppose, for example, that we are droning along happily at, say, 70 knots, when we suddenly run into a downdraught which, to a first order, demands a speed of 85 knots according to the MacCready ring. On increasing speed to 85 knots, the rate of sink of the sailplane has increased and we are now required to fly at 90 knots. But, on increasing speed to 90 knots, there is a further increase in the rate of sink, and so on. In practice, one learns to overshoot a little, and in any case, the external conditions are unlikely to remain steady, so that the above scenario cannot be precisely reproduced. However, it would be nice if it were not lurking in the background, so to speak, thus complicating an already somewhat awkward process.

The difficulty is that the variometer continues to show the rate of sink of the sailplane and it is the variation in this quantity which causes bother. In order to remove this quantity from the indications of the variometer a leak is applied to the bottle side of the variometer, via a capillary tube as in Fig. 9.4. Now the rate of flow through the capillary will be proportional to the pressure difference between the ends, assuming laminar flow in the capillary, and that pressure difference will be the dynamic head, $\frac{1}{2}\rho V^2$. If the rate of sink of the sailplane were parabolic, then the compensation system of Fig. 9.4 could be arranged to operate exactly but, of course, the performance curve is not parabolic. However, the errors, over the useful part of the curve, can be arranged to be very small. Appendix 7 of "New Soaring Pilot" suggests a theoretical approach to this matter, but in practice there are so many uncertainties that it is best to arrange an empirical calibration. Starting from the idea that the capillary will be about 12" long if the internal diameter is 0.0145", a series of flights are made when the air is totally calm, the variometer being connected as shown in Fig. 9.4. The length of the tube is adjusted until the variometer reads zero at some reasonable speed, such as 70 knots, but it will then be found that it also reads close to zero at all likely cruise speeds. Since the pressure drop along such a capillary is inversely proportional to the fourth power of the diameter and to its length, it will be appreciated that small manufacturing errors can make a very large difference to the final length. Of course, different lengths of capillary will be required for different maximum weights of the sailplane and the ring is calibrated by putting the speed markings opposite values of the rate of climb, V_c, on the variometer scale.

An extension of this system enables the variometer to be used as a flight path indicator. If the capillary tube is shorter than that corresponding to that of the Air Mass Movement, or "net" variometer, then when the sailplane is descending, the rate of flow through the capillary will be greater than the rate of flow into the bottle. There will therefore be an outflow through the variometer, which will show some rate of climb reading. It is possible to arrange the capillary leak so that, whatever the motions of the atmosphere, the sailplane is being flown at the correct speed if the climb reading is kept constant. The length of the capillary is about one-third of that required by the previous system and the ring is now very simple: it consists of a datum mark to be set to the estimated rate of climb and a single mark at some suitable circumferential distance from the datum. Further information is given in "New Soaring Pilot", but the widespread use of electrical instruments has rendered such mechanical contrivances largely obsolete.

Corrections to the Variometer

We have previously noted that in order to make a MacCready ring work properly, both the vertical and horizontal speeds should either be "true" or "equivalent". In practice, one is faced with an ASI giving something close to EAS and a variometer which, if mechanical, will show a vertical speed in terms of something close to TAS, or if electric, something like TAS $\times \rho$. In either case, there is a mismatch. For example, at a height of 10,000 ft, a mechanical variometer will show about 16% too much. So, if we were flying with an equivalent rate of climb of 2.64 knots at 10,000 ft, the speed we ought to be flying at is 75 knots. However, the rate of climb shown on the variometer is 3.072 knots, corresponding to an EAS of 77.5 knots. This is only 2.5 knots too much, which might be thought negligible. However, it corresponds to spending 45% of one's time in thermals, as opposed to 43%. This may not seem much, but the effect increases with altitude and why spend any more time in thermals than is strictly necessary?

This snag could be avoided by having a suitable electric device, which essentially uses EAS for everything, except navigation. The manufacturers of such devices are inclined to be a little vague about what they actually use, so some of them may only be correct at sea-level.

In general, we need to be rather wary about the indications of the MacCready ring and similar devices. Many a person has found an initial thermal, found it to have a rate of climb of about 5 knots, and has then rushed off at about 88 knots straight into a field landing. All of this could have been avoided if he had surveyed the scene from the top of the first thermal, and then decided on a reasonable speed to fly to get to the next visible thermal (if it's that sort of day) and then only working up to the speeds shown on the ring when the thermals are regular.

If the sailplane is fitted with flaps, each flap setting corresponds to a different polar. However, the optimum envelope usually corresponds quite closely to Eq. (4.12), and therefore all of the previous constructions and/or calculations can be used, assuming that the machine is always flown at the optimum flap setting.

So far, we have said nothing about the wind. On a straightforward cross-country flight, the wind affects the navigation and the final glide, as considered in Chapter 12. All we need say here is that the wind has no effect on the optimum speed for gliding between thermals since the glides and climbs are all taking place in an air mass moving bodily over the countryside, and conditions for a maximum speed through the air are also the conditions for maximum speed over the ground. The wind will obviously affect the speed attained over the ground and the height to leave the last thermal of the flight. This assumes that the thermals are convected with the wind, which seems a reasonable state of affairs, but some sources of lift remain more-or-less stationary with respect to the ground. Lee waves are one example, to be considered in Chapter 12.

References

The material of this chapter has been taken, with suitable modifications to take into account the passage of time, from:

Welch, A. & L. and Irving, F.G., *New Soaring Pilot*, John Murray, London, 1977.

Chapter 10

MORE ADVANCED IDEAS ON CROSS-COUNTRY FLYING

In the last chapter, we considered the use of the MacCready ring and in Chapter 8 we noted that some analyses used a climb-glide sequence whilst others used the glide-climb. At an elementary stage, both analyses are quite valid. But in 1978, Messrs. Litt and Sander published an analysis of cross-country flights which, although it still had many unrealistic features, gave some useful rules.

Their assumptions were as follows:

1. Thermals are concentrated at places unequally spaced along the trajectory.
2. Their locations and characteristics do not change with time.
3. Their strengths are generally unequal.
4. The air between them is still.
5. There may be upper and lower bounds to the operating heights.
6. The sailplane is flown at constant speed between the thermals.
7. There is no wind.
8. The flight begins and ends at a given minimum height.
9. Each glide is linear but all glides are not necessarily in the same direction.

The pilot has to decide how far to climb in each thermal and the speed to fly between them. The object is to maximise the overall speed for the task. Various sets of rules can be deduced, which depend on the assumed height constraints. There will usually be a lower height limit, below which the pilot gives up soaring and resigns himself to landing, and similarly an upper limit, above which the rate of climb

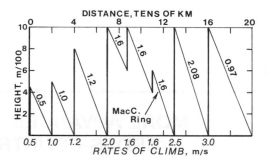

Fig. 10.1. A cross-country flight to illustrate the theory of Litt and Sander.

becomes unacceptably low or cloudbase or controlled airspace intervenes. The author considered four cases, of which the first two were not very relevant. The first assumed no height constraints at all and therefore leads to the "classical" analysis and the simple use of the MacCready ring. The second assumes a minimum but no maximum altitude constraint and leads to some odd-looking rules, since one can always climb high enough to reach the first of the next thermals stronger than the first one, flying at the MacCready speed appropriate to the first thermal, and so on. More realistic is the third case, where there are both maximum and minimum altitude constraints. A short section of such a flight is shown in Fig. 10.1, where the thermal spacings are at mutiples of 10 km, simply for ease of drawing, and it will be noted that the speed during a glide is sometimes appropriate to the strength of the preceding thermal, sometimes to that of the next thermal, and sometimes to neither. Incidentally, the analysis of such flights invokes the Calculus of Variations, a topic which is touched upon in Chapter 11. This produced a set of rules of some complexity, which were simplified by de Jong (1982), as follows:

A. In any thermal, climb only high enough to reach a stronger thermal at minimum altitude by flying with a MacCready ring setting corresponding to the present climb rate.
B. If there is no stronger thermal that can be reached using Rule A, climb to maximum altitude and proceed with the highest feasible

MacCready ring setting with which a thermal can be reached, at or above the minimum height, having a climb rate equal to or larger than that corresponding to the MacCready ring setting.

The rules for the final glide are then as follows:

A′. In the last thermal, climb only high enough to reach the finish at the minimum safety altitude by flying with a MacCready ring setting corresponding to the climb rate in the last thermal.

B′. If the finish cannot be reached by following Rule A′; climb to maximum altitude and proceed with the highest feasible MacCready ring setting at which the finish can be reached at the minimum safety altitude.

(These rules have been slightly paraphrased, but only to make them more readable). In a more complicated case, the strength of each thermal varies with height, with an initial increase in strength followed by a decrease: altitude constraints are implicit in such a distribution of strength. The rules are then as follows:

1. The MacCready ring setting must correspond to the instantaneous rate of climb at the height of leaving the thermal.
2. The rate of climb at the height of encountering the next thermal must be the same as that on leaving the previous thermal.
3. If this procedure is not possible, proceed as in Par. B′ above.

For a pair of thermals with given distributions of climb rate, at a certain distance apart, these rules lead to a unique solution, which gives the height to leave the first thermal, the speed to glide and the height to meet the second thermal, as shown in Fig. 10.2. These rules appear in Reichmann's book (1978) and had been deduced by a process of Pure Thought by Anthony Edwards some years earlier (1964). This, of course, represents an ideal state of affairs almost impossible to achieve in real life. Fortunately, the variation of rate of climb with height is usually rather different from that shown in Fig. 10.2, having a reasonably lengthy constant region in the middle, so the advice is that it usually pays to leave the thermal as soon as the rate of climb starts to fall off. Then, assuming that on a given day, thermals are sufficiently abundant, and

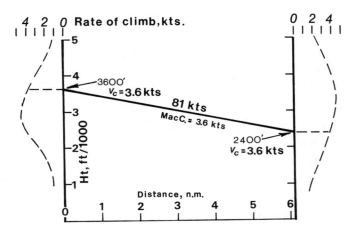

Fig. 10.2. A flight between thermals of varying strength.

have roughly the same strength, the MacCready ring setting will correspond to that strength.

Although Litt and Sanders assume still air between the thermals, one can assume that down-draughts degrade the performance by an amount that is roughly constant, although it may vary slowly with the time of day. So, it seems reasonable to follow the indications of the MacCready ring, having set it in accordance with the foregoing rules.

Dolphin Flying

So far, all of the theory including the classical "best speed to fly theory" assumes a load factor of unity, or something quite close to this figure. But, in following the indications of the MacCready ring, we wish to increase speed where the air is descending and to slow down where it is ascending, and the theory implicitly assumes that such speed changes can be made instantaneously. Obviously, this is not possible, but how rapidly should the speed changes be made?

The matter of encountering an up-draught was considered by Gorisch (1981), with a wealth of vector analysis. This ultimately amounts to the following: in normal steady flight in still air we are accustomed to the

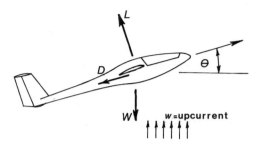

Fig. 10.3. Flying in an up-current.

lift vector acting at right angles to the direction of motion, and it therefore does no work. When flying in an up-draught (see Fig. 10.3), with initially θ assumed zero, the lift is no longer at right angles to the direction of motion: indeed it is being convected upwards at a velocity w and therefore does work at the rate Lw, which equals nWw if the load factor is n. Now the work done is equal to the weight multiplied by the rate of change of energy height plus the instantaneous rate of sink. So we get:

$$W\left[dh_e/dt + V_s\right] = nWw$$

or

$$dh_e/dt = nw - V_s. \tag{10.1}$$

Under the conditions shown in the diagram, the effective up-draught becomes $w\cos\theta$, and since the load factor is no longer unity, the drag depends on both the speed and the load factor. So finally, the general expression of this equation is:

$$dh_e/dt = nw\cos\theta - V_s\left(V, n\right). \tag{10.2}$$

This leads to some curious conclusions. Effectively, the strength of an up-current is multiplied by the load factor, provided the increase in drag is not excessive, and energy can also be extracted from a down-current, by applying a negative load factor. Clearly, applying a positive load factor in sinking air or a negative load factor in rising air is not a good idea. For a given sailplane, there will be a load factor depending on the forward speed and the rate of ascent of the air, which maximises the rate of gain of energy height. The optimum value is quite high: for a Standard Class sailplane at 80 knots, meeting an up-current of 4 knots, the optimum load factor is about 4.88. Such load factors, apart from being very emetic, can only be sustained for very short periods: even at a load factor of 3.0 and an initial speed of 80 knots, the machine is pointing vertically upwards after 3.5 sec. With $\theta = 90°$, the amplification due to the increased load factor becomes zero anyway, so in practice, something rather gentler is required.

However, the effect is perfectly real and it is possible to perform more complex calculations to see how one should fly in more complicated situations. For example, Pierson and Chen (1979) have applied another dose of the Calculus of Variations to considering a sailplane flying (1) through a sinusoidal pattern of vertical motions of the atmosphere with a wavelength of 1000 m and (2) with a wavelength of 500 m, with zero height loss in both cases. In the first case, the result, as one would expect, is quite close to the classical one: one slows down in the up-current and speeds up in the down-current. But in the second case, the opposite is true, in order to apply a significant positive load factor in the up-current and a negative load factor in the down-current. At some intermediate wavelength, it doesn't matter which trajectory is used. There are, it is worth saying, numerous other papers on this subject. Gorisch (1981) has achieved some tentative rules, as follows:

1. Adjust the *average speed* according to the speed command of the MacCready ring fitted to an *averaging* total energy variometer.
2. Perform load variations according to the *instantaneous* variometer reading. The speed varies, but its average should be maintained according to the previous rule.

The Carriage of Water Ballast

A little thought shows that it pays to make provision for the carriage of a great deal of water ballast. Speeds, both along the flight path and vertically, are proportional to the square root of the all-up weight and hence the carriage of say 100 lb of water in a machine initially weighing

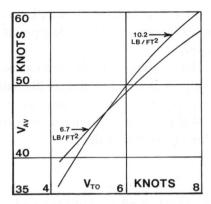

Fig. 10.4. The performance of the ASW-24 in thermals of 1000 ft radius and different core strengths at two different wing loadings.

700 lb will make very little difference. This was the order of things before the war, when it was realised that adding weight would improve the performance in strong conditions, but there was little guide as to how much water was required. As is not unusual, an element of compromise is involved: the carriage of ballast gives higher speeds for the same glide angle, but the rate of sink in thermals is increased and so is the radius of turn for a given angle of bank. We can, for example, consider flight in parabolic thermals of the usual standard English radius, taken to be 1000 ft., and with core velocities up to 8 knots. We can consider a machine with a wing loading of 6.7 lb/sq ft and the polar of Fig. 8.4, approximately that of the ASW-24. We proceed as for finding the handicap, that is to say, we find the optimum angle of bank and hence the maximum rate of climb for a variety of thermal strengths using Eqs. (8.1) and (8.2), and from Table 9.1 we can find the maximum overall average speed. Then we can repeat all of this for some greater wing loading, say 10.2 lb/ft^2. The results are as shown in Fig. 10.4, from which it will be observed, that the lower wing loading is better up to a thermal core strength of about 5.4 knots and the higher wing loading in stronger thermals. However, this is only one sort of thermal: it might reasonably be expected that the radius of the thermal would increase with increasing core strength, which would give a cross-over point at a

lower strength. So, on a decent-looking day, be advised that it always pays to start with water: it can always be dumped if the thermals do not come up to expectations.

Also be advised that it pays to look rather closely at the limitations placard before pouring in as much water as the sailplane will take. On some machines, it is quite easy to exceed the Maximum Permitted weight with water, and this will cause the maximum spar stress outboard of the ends of the water bags to be exceeded.

References

Edwards, A.W.F., "The arm-chair pilot", *Sailplane and Gliding*, October, 1964.

Gorisch, W., "Load variation style and its implications to the theory of soaring", *OSTIV Publication* **XVI**, 1981.

De Jong, J.L., *"How glider pilots get there faster"*, Letter to *Sailplane and Gliding*, October/November, 1982 and reply by F.G. Irving.

Litt, F.X. and Sander, G., "Optimal flight strategy in a given space-distribution of lifts with minimum and maximum altitude constraints", *OSTIV Publication* **XV**, 1978.

Pierson, B.L. and Chen, I., "Minimum time soaring through a specified vertical wind distribution", Presented at the *9th IFIP conference on Optimum-Techniques*, Warsaw, September, 1979.

Reichmann, H., *Cross-Country Soaring*, Thomson Publications, 1978.

Chapter 11

OPTIMISATIONS IN GENERAL

The Calculus of Variations

There are many problems such as those discussed in Chapter 8 where we wish to find the value of a variable which causes a function of the variable to have a "stationary" value. For example, we may wish to find the value of the inter-thermal speed which makes the overall speed a maximum. This type of problem represents a straightforward application of ordinary calculus.

There is, however, a class of problems of greater complexity. In such a case, we wish to find the stationary values of an integral with respect to a function, possibly with other limitations superimposed. A simple example of such a problem is the "brachistochrone" of Euler. Two points, A and B, A being higher than B, are to be connected by a curve lying in a vertical plane through A and B. What should be the shape of the curve such that a frictionless particle moving along the curve under the influence of gravity traverses the path AB in the shortest time? Here, the function is the shape of the curve and the integral is the time to traverse the curve. (The answer is that the curve should be a cycloid.)

This type of problem lies within the scope of the Calculus of Variations, which is generally more complicated than ordinary calculus. Many of the problems concerning flight paths, particularly those relating to supersonic flight (Miele and Cappellari, 1959), require its application and soaring is no exception despite the low Mach numbers. Thus a likely problem might be as follows: consider an expanse of countryside in which are to be found thermals of various strengths and various

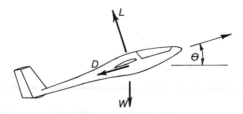

Fig. 11.1. The sailplane at some general moment in a flight.

height limits. What is the best strategy to fly from one point to another in the least time? It is by no means clear whether one flies reasonably straight, accepting some poor thermals and occasionally having to glide at the speed for maximum L/D, or whether one zig-zags to use better thermals. In fact this sort of problem is generally insoluble, since in real life its solution requires powers of prophecy, although some approximate rules can be formulated. It is also clear that some effort goes into simplifying the problems so that they can be dealt with by the rules of ordinary calculus and to reduce the element of foresight required.

It is not the author's intention to provide a comprehensive guide to the Calculus of Variations, but it leads to an important general result and at least one neat application: that of cloud-street flying.

Analysis of the Best Speed to Fly

Figure 11.1 shows the sailplane at some general moment in a flight on a constant heading. Let x denote the distance along the flight path and w (positive upwards) the local vertical velocity of the air. To an external observer, w will be a function of both distance x and time t, but from the point of view of the pilot, it may be regarded as a function of x only. Suppose that the instantaneous forward speed of the sailplane is V. Also assume that the air density is substantially constant.

The time to travel from x_1 to x_2 will be:

$$T = \int_{x_2}^{x_1} dx/V \ .$$

The equation of motion of the sailplane along its flight path in still air will be:

$$D + W \sin\theta + (W/g)\, dV/dt = 0, \tag{11.1}$$

where θ is positive nose-up (see Fig. 11.1).

If the energy height is h_e, where

$$h_e = h + V^2/2g,$$

and h is the true height, then

$$h_e/dt = dh/dt + (V/g)\, dV/dt = V \sin\theta + (V/g)\, dV/dt,$$

and from (11.1),

$$dh_e/dt = -DV/W.$$

But DV/W is the rate of sink of the sailplane, V_s, when flying steadily at speed V.

In the presence of an up-current w the total rate of change of energy height will be

$$(dh_e/dt)_{\text{tot}} = w - V_s. \tag{11.2}$$

This, of course, assumes that the load factor is substantially unity: otherwise we must use the expression from Chapter 10 and the problem becomes too complicated.

The total change of energy height between x_1 and x_2 will be:

$$H_e = \int_{x_2}^{x_1} (dh_e/dt)_{\text{tot}} \, (dt/dx) \, dx$$

$$= \int_{x_2}^{x_1} (w - V_s)\,(1/V)\, dx$$

Now let us suppose that we wish to fly in such a fashion that, for a given $(x_1 - x_2)$, T is a minimum and $H_e = 0$. This is not the only criterion which could be applied, but it seems to be a simple and likely case.

$$T \text{ is of the form } \int F(V)dx \text{ and}$$

$$H_e \text{ is of the form } \int G(V, x)dx.$$

It therefore follows from the Calculus of Variations that the criterion to be satisfied is

$$\partial F^*/\partial V = 0,$$

$$\text{where } F^* = F + \lambda G$$

$$= (1/V) + (\lambda/V)(w - V_s),\qquad(11.3)$$

and λ is a constant Lagrange multiplier. The precise significance of a Lagrange multiplier is not of much significance in this analysis: it is simply to be regarded as a constant for each particular problem.

So the criterion is:

$$-(1/V^2) - (\lambda/V^2)(w - V_s) - (\lambda/V)(\partial V_s/\partial V) = 0.\qquad(11.4)$$

since V_s is a function of V only.

This can be re-arranged to give:

$$\partial V_s/\partial V = (V_s - w - (1/\lambda))/V,$$

or, since $(1/\lambda)$ must clearly have the dimension of velocity,

$$\partial V_s/\partial V = (V_s - w - w^*)/V.\qquad(11.5)$$

The criterion expressed by this last equation is shown graphically in Fig. 11.2.

This is, in fact, the "classical" construction. It is noteworthy that we have only specified that the speed should be a maximum and the total change of energy height should be zero: the nature of the lift, be it normal thermals or cloud streets or waves is not defined. It defines, in effect, the zero-setting of the MacCready ring and whilst the diagram is drawn for a positive value of w^*, its actual value remains to be determined by the circumstances of the problem.

What we can say is as follows: **any problem which involves finding the best speed to fly so that the overall speed is a maximum and**

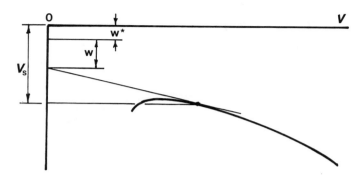

Fig. 11.2. The criterion for maximum speed.

the total change of energy height is zero, the load factor being substantially unity, is solved by drawing a tangent to the polar. The point from which the tangent is to be drawn remains to be defined, according to the nature of the problem.

This is the sort of problem which can be solved by a suitable setting of the MacCready ring, or setting an appropriate rate of climb on an electrical device, since $w + w^*$ is essentially the zero setting of the ring. It should be noted that this total quantity will often be negative: indeed circumstances may arise when one should fly at a speed less than that for minimum rate of sink: it may be advantageous to spend a long time in a feeble up-current at the expense of some increase in the rate of sink.

From the pilot's point of view, this analysis contains a difficulty: w^* is ultimately determined by the condition that $H_e = 0$, and hence requires a knowledge of w as a function of x over the distance $x_2 - x_1$. Unfortunately, as remarked elsewhere, prophecy is in rather short supply amongst soaring pilots. When flying under a cloud street, the pilot may initially wish to gain height, on the average, until he is reasonably close to cloud base, and then adjust the MacCready ring by a process of successive approximation so that, overall, there is no net change of height. In real life there tends to be insufficient time to make such adjustments other than very approximately.

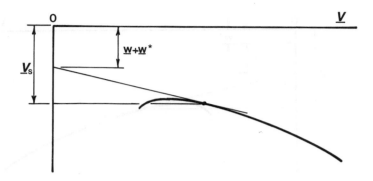

Fig. 11.3. The dimensionless criterion for maximum speed.

Example of an Unflapped Sailplane Flying Under a Cloud Street

In Eq. (4.12), we saw that the dimensionless expression for the idealised performance curve was:

$$2V_{si}/V_{sio} = (V_i/V_{io})^3 + (V_{io}/V).$$

Now, if we denote V_{si}/V_{sio} by $\underline{V}_s$ and V_i/V_{io} by $\underline{V}$, then this may equally be written

$$\underline{V}_s = \tfrac{1}{2}\left(\underline{V}^3 + 1/\underline{V}\right). \tag{11.6}$$

Let $\underline{w} = w/V_{sio}$ and $\underline{w}^* = w^*/V_{sio}$. Then, in dimensionless terms, the criterion of Eq. (11.5) becomes

$$\partial\underline{V}_s/\partial\underline{V} = \left(\underline{V}_s - \underline{w} - \underline{w}^*\right)/\underline{V}, \tag{11.7}$$

and this is illustrated in Fig. 11.3.

From (11.6) and (11.7)

$$\tfrac{1}{2}\left(3\underline{V}^2 - 1/\underline{V}^2\right) = \tfrac{1}{2}\left(\underline{V}^2 - 1/\underline{V}^2\right) - \left(\underline{w} + \underline{w}^*\right)/\underline{V}, \tag{11.8}$$

which becomes

$$\underline{w} + \underline{w}^* = (1/\underline{V}) - \underline{V}^3. \tag{11.9}$$

Suppose that a distance x_1, in which the upwards velocity of the air has a constant value w, is covered at an optimum speed V_1 and a distance x_2, in which $w = 0$, is covered at the corresponding optimum speed V_2. Then, from (11.9),

$$\underline{w} + \underline{w}^* = (1/\underline{V}_1) - \underline{V}_1^3 \tag{11.10}$$

and

$$\underline{w}^* = (1/\underline{V}_2) - \underline{V}_2^3, \tag{11.11}$$

whence

$$\underline{w} = (1/\underline{V}_1) - \underline{V}_1^3 - (1/\underline{V}_2) + \underline{V}_2^3. \tag{11.12}$$

Also, the rate of climb over the distance x_1 will be $V_c = w - V_{s1}$. For zero overall height change:

$$x_1 \underline{V}_c/\underline{V}_1 = x_2 \underline{V}_{s2}/\underline{V}_2. \tag{11.13}$$

Strictly, since the previous theory dealt with energy heights rather than true heights, this expression should include a kinetic energy correction, omitted here in the interests of simplicity. So

$$x_1/x_2 = (\underline{V}_{s2}/\underline{V}_2)[V_1/(\underline{w} - \underline{V}_{s1})]. \tag{11.14}$$

Since $\underline{V}_{s1}$ and $\underline{V}_{s2}$ are functions of $\underline{V}_1$ and $\underline{V}_2$ respectively, (11.13) and (11.14) can, in principle, be solved simultaneously to give $\underline{V}_1$ and $\underline{V}_2$ if $\underline{w}$ and x_1/x_2 are known.

It is interesting to consider what combinations of thermal strength ($\underline{w}$, in effect) and distance ratio x_1/x_2 are required to maintain continuous flight. One obvious particular case occurs when $\underline{V}_2/\underline{V}_{s2}$ is a maximum (i.e., when the sailplane is flown at $(L/D)_{max}$ over the distance x_2). This will correspond to $\underline{V}_2 = 1$, $\underline{V}_{s2} = 1$.

Under these conditions, from (11.11), (11.10) and (11.14):

$$\underline{w}^* = 0,$$

$$\underline{w} = (1/\underline{V}_1) - \underline{V}_1^3 \tag{11.15}$$

$$x_1/x_2 = 2\underline{V}_1^2/(1 - 3\underline{V}_1^4) \tag{11.16}$$

Eliminating V_1 from (11.15) and (11.16) gives a relation between and w the least value of x_1/x_2 which will just permit continuous flight. It is apparent that $V_1^4 < \frac{1}{3}$, from (11.16). Now, from (11.6), this case corresponds to $V_{s\min}$, so, as is apparent on physical grounds, the limiting case corresponds to flying at minmum sink in a continuous up-current of the same strength, i.e., $x_1/x_2 = \infty$, $w = V_{s1} = (\frac{2}{3})^{\frac{3}{4}}$

The choice of values of V_1 is therefore very limited: the maximum value is $3^{-0.25}$ and the minimum value is that corresponding to the stall.

These results are not very realistic: because we have imposed the condition that the average speed shall be a maximum, very weak thermals require the sailplane to be flown at unrealistically low speeds. The expression used for the performance, (11.6), has no implied lower limit to V. It would be better to assume that the sailplane is never flown at a speed less than that corresponding to minimum sink, in which case in examining the limiting conditions for continuous flight, we abandon the maximum average concept. The sailplane is flown at minimum rate of sink in the rising air and at its best gliding angle in the still air.

Inserting $V_2 = V_{s2} = 1$, $V_1 = 3^{-0.25}$ and $V_{s1} = (\frac{2}{3})^{\frac{3}{4}}$ in (11.14), this becomes approximately,

$$x_1/x_2 = 0.759/(w - 0.878). \qquad (11.17)$$

Figures obtained from Eq. (11.17) are given in Table 11.1:

Table 11.1

w	$x_1/(x_1 + x_2)$
0.878	1
1.0	0.86
2.0	0.403
3.0	0.272
4.0	0.196
5.0	0.155
6.0	0.129
7.0	0.110
8.0	0.096

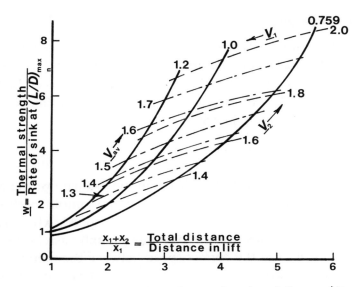

Fig. 11.4. A plot of speeds against thermal strength and total distance/distance in lift, all in dimensionless terms, for flight under a cloud street.

In this table, w = thermal strength/rate of sink of the sailplane at maximum L/D, $x_1/(x_1 + x_2)$ = distance in rising air/total distance.

If we now consider in general terms the case of achieving maximum average speed, we can assign some likely constant value to V_1 and then consider a series of values of V_2. From Eq. (11.12) we can obtain the value of w. Since V_{s1} and V_{s2} are simply related to V_1 and V_2 respectively, we can obtain x_1/x_2, or more usefully $(x_1 + x_2)/x_1$ from Eq. (11.14). It is then possible to find the dimensionless cross-country speed, V_{av}, since

$$V_{av} = (x_1 V_1 + x_2 V_2)/(x_1 + x_2). \tag{11.18}$$

For the present purposes, the assumed values of V_1 were 0.759 (i.e., the speed for minimum rate of sink), 1.0 (speed for best gliding angle) and 1.2. Values of V_2 up to 2.0 were taken. The results are presented in Fig. 11.4.

A Numerical Example

Consider a sailplane whose $(L/D)_{max}$ is 43 at 58 knots EAS. If $\underline{w} = 4$ over 25% of the flight path, the upcurrent strength would be $4 \times 58/43$, i.e., 5.395 knots. Flown at $\underline{V}_1 = 0.759$, the rate of climb would be $5.395 - 0.878 \times 58/43 = 4.211$ knots. $\underline{V}_2$ is then 1.57 or 91.06 knots, and the average speed becomes 1.36×58 or 78.88 knots.

A Final Caution

The above analysis will give an optimistic estimate of the average speed, since it assumes in Eq. (11.6) that the simple performance expression applies down to the minimum sink speed, which is rather unlikely. Also, it assumes that the pilot can instantly assess the overall situation, and will fly at the correct speed between the thermals. It also assumes a "square wave" pattern for the lift and no downcurrents between the lift, both of which are most unlikely. So, altogether, there are many simplifying guesses, but it does indicate that the speeds attained are likely to be considerably higher than can be attained in normal thermal soaring. In practice, one would fly at the speed of minimum sink in the lift, or perhaps a little slower, and it will then be necessary to experiment in the bits of the cloud street between the lifting sections, trying to obtain that compromise between a high speed without losing height on the average.

References

Much of the material in this chapter is taken from:

Irving, F.G., "Cloud-street flying", *NASA Contractor Report*, NASA CR-2315, November, 1973.

Also relevant and interesting is:

Miele, A. and Cappellari, J.O., "Approximate solutions to optimum flight trajectories for a turbojet-powered aircraft", *NASA Tech. Note D-152*, September, 1959.

Chapter 12

THE EFFECTS OF WIND

So far, we have implicitly assumed that the wind is zero. In practice, zero wind rarely occurs and it has a profound effect on almost all aspects of cross-country flying. A good example is the calculation of the height to leave the last thermal of a flight, for which the starting point is to assume that the wind is, in fact, zero (see Fig. 12.1). If the strength of the last thermal was constant, then the speed during the final glide would be that corresponding to this value according to the classical theory. The calculation of the final glide and the height to leave the last thermal is therefore simple: if the best speed is V_{opt} and the distance to go is X, then the time taken will be X/V_{opt} and if the rate of sink at V_{opt} is V_s, then the height to leave the last thermal will be $X V_s/V_{opt}$. This assumes no safety allowance, so far as height is concerned, so a prudent height would have to be assumed at point C.

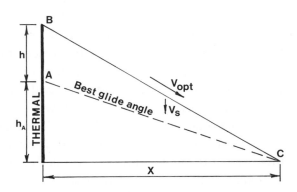

Fig. 12.1. Height to leave the last thermal in zero wind when the thermal strength is constant.

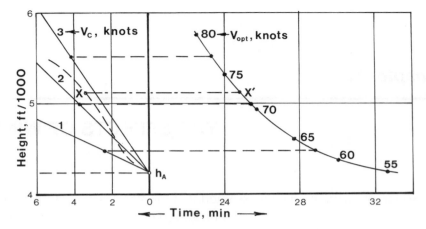

Fig. 12.2. Height to leave the last thermal when its strength is variable.

Now, whilst climbing in the last thermal, a height h_A will eventually be attained from which the goal can just be attained by flying at maximum L/D. It will then be possible to leave the thermal at any greater height and achieve the goal with little trouble. The problem is now to minimise the time for the path ABC, recognising that the strength of the thermal may be variable. Now consider Fig. 12.2, in which the somewhat irregular line on the left represents the thermal. Since the plot is on a height-time basis, showing heights above A, then the thermal strength is indicated by the gradient of this line. The line on the right is a plot of gliding speed, giving the gliding time in minutes to cover the required distance. At any particular height above A, the glide angle to reach the goal will be known, and hence the speed, given the performance of the sailplane. The distance between the line representing the thermal and that representing the glide will be proportional to the total time of the flight once point A has been achieved, and hence we wish to fly in such a fashion as to make this time a minimum. This will correspond to the line XX′, and the gradients of the curves at X and X′ will be the same. Putting it another way, the pilot continues to climb until the rate of climb no longer exceeds that appropriate to the speed at which the glider could be flown to the goal at that instant, the relation between climb rate and speed being that of the classical theory. An interesting

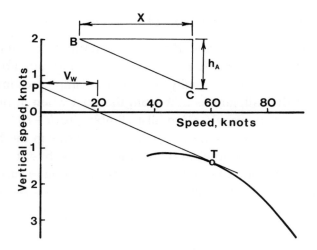

Fig. 12.3. Criterion for gliding to the goal from height h_A or greater in a thermal of constant stength with a headwind.

feature of this situation is that the pilot is now interested in the instantaneous rate of climb, rather than some average rate of climb. So, in the example shown, if the rate of climb is 3 knots at a height of 4,500 ft, the pilot goes on climbing, but if the rate of climb falls off to 2.3 knots at, say, 5,100 ft, he stops climbing, sets the MacCready ring to 2.3 knots and departs for his goal. This situation has the advantage that if an unforeseen down- or up-draught occurs, the pilot can always regulate his speed accordingly.

In the presence of a wind, the situation becomes markedly more complicated. Again, there is a height h_A from which the pilot can just reach the goal at a distance X, but the minimum gliding speed is now given by the construction of Fig. 12.3. Extrapolating the tangent to the left to intersect the vertical axis implies that this situation corresponds to a certain thermal strength, that which causes the glider to climb whilst drifting downwind, always just able to reach the goal. (This is written as if there is a headwind component: similar considerations will apply to a tailwind, with the signs reversed.) The expression for calculating the height required is now

$$(h + h_A)/(X + hV_w/V_c) = V_s/(V_{opt} - V_w) \tag{12.1}$$

from which it will be inferred that the optimum speed remains that given by the classical theory, a result which would require about a page of mathematics to display formally. This relationship takes into account the fact that, if the sailplane is at X from the goal when at height h_A, it will drift back a distance hV_w/V_c whilst climbing to $h + h_A$.

Obviously, trying to do these sorts of calculations in the heat of the moment is quite impossible, and in practice one has to resort to a calculator. This can either be of the mechanical analogue variety or, in a modern sailplane, a suitable electronic device.

Wind Components

In the above theory, we have considered a headwind component or, with a sign change, a tailwind. But in most circumstances, the wind will be directed at some angle to the desired track and we will will wish to assess its effect. Suppose that V is the true airspeed of the sailplane, either the average over a long task or the gliding speed if we are only concerned with a single glide. From the triangle of velocities, the speed made good along the track will be

$$V_{tr} = V \cos\lambda - V_w \cos\gamma \tag{12.2}$$

where λ is the angle between the course and the track and γ is the angle between the wind direction and the track. But since

$$V \sin\lambda = V_w \sin\gamma \tag{12.3}$$

λ may be eliminated from Eqs. (12.2) and (12.3) to give

$$V_{tr} = V\left[1 - (V_w/V)^2 \sin^2\gamma\right]^{\frac{1}{2}} - V_w \cos\gamma. \tag{2.4}$$

The effective headwind is then the difference between the speed of the sailplane and the speed made good along the track, i.e.,

$$V_{weff} = V - V_{tr} = V\left[1 - \left(1 - (V_w/V)^2 \sin^2\gamma\right)^{\frac{1}{2}} + (V_w/V)\cos\gamma\right]. \tag{12.5}$$

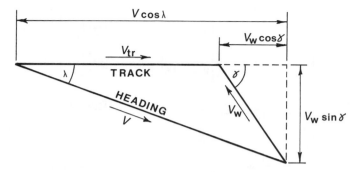

Fig. 12.4. Triangle of velocities, in the general case.

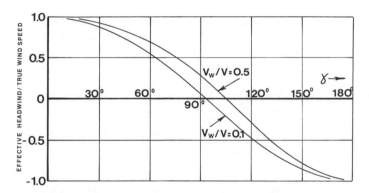

Fig. 12.5. The effective headwind plotted against the orientation of the task, for two values of the headwind.

A consequence of this expression is that a wind at right angles to the track reduces the speed made good along the track, although it has no component in the direction of the track. This effect arises because the sailplane must proceed on a course which is slightly into wind in order that its resultant track shall be in the correct direction. (See Fig. 12.4).

Figure 12.5 shows plots of V_{weff}/V_w against γ for two values of V_w/V. It will be seen that when $V_w/V = 0.5$, the effective headwind only becomes zero when γ is about $104°$. A consequence of this situation is that, in closed-circuit tasks, the effects of wind are never self-cancelling. For straight out-and-return tasks conducted at a constant average true

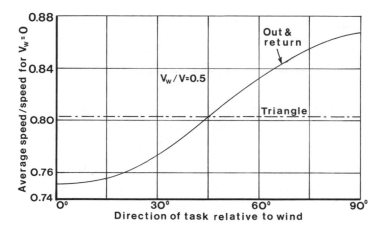

Fig. 12.6. Average speed plotted against orientation of the task, for one wind speed. Note that whilst the effect on the triangle is here shown as constant, and is referred to as such in the text, there is, in fact, a very small variation in speed.

airspeed, the direction of the task relative to the wind has very little influence on the total time if the wind is light. But if the wind is strong, the highest average speed is attained when the task is cross-wind. Figure 12.6 is derived from the previous plot and shows average speeds for the case $V_w/V = 0.5$, relative to the zero-wind case for various orientations of the task. The cross-wind task is about 15% faster than the upwind and downwind tasks. For closed-circuit tasks consisting of equilateral triangles, the orientation of a task relative to the wind direction has no effect.

So far, we have assumed that the average true airspeed is constant throughout the flight. If the thermals are of constant strength, the final leg of a closed circuit task will be the fastest because, if the task is started at a height of say 1000 m, then the final glide from 1000 m down to ground level can be regarded as a bonus since it is flown at the optimum gliding speed, appreciably faster than the average speed of the flight. This effect has some influence on the optimum orientation of a task in the presence of a wind.

Consider a flight of 300 km in which the optimum gliding speed between thermals is 80 knots and the corresponding average speed is

46 knots. If the wind is 13.8 knots, then the average value of V_w/V will be 0.3 and, at 80 knots, it will be 0.1725. It is assumed that the final glide starts from 1000 m. Hence, from the preceding theory, we can work out the time for the two legs of an out-and-return flight, the second including the final glide. The average speeds for the two legs are then as follows:

(a) First leg downwind: 44.42 knots
(b) First leg upwind: 43.21 knots
(c) Both legs crosswind: 45.98 knots
(d) In zero wind: 48.14 knots

So, it will be seen that a downwind final leg leads to the lowest average speed. Given complete freedom of choice, one would wish to make both legs crosswind, but the direction of a flight is usually governed by other considerations. It then pays to make the first leg as nearly downwind as possible.

Similarly, one can analyse a triangular flight, leading to the conclusion that, for equilateral triangles, the last leg downwind leads to the lowest average speed and the first leg downwind gives the highest. Of course, this assumes that the thermals are of constant strength throughout the day: if they are initially feeble, this will affect the above results and may well reverse them. But in any case, the results for a 100 km flight will be greatly exaggerated compared with those quoted above. In such a situation, it would certainly pay to think about the direction of the flight, and to make the start height as great as possible in the light of whatever rules prevail.

Optimum Glide Angles

If the pilot is concerned with the best gliding angle through the air, as when trying to reach a distant cloud, then the best speed to fly will correspond to point L on the performance curve (see Fig. 12.7) where L corresponds to the best gliding angle. In other words, one sets the MacCready ring to zero, and then obeys its readings if the atmosphere is not steady. But circumstances may arise in which the pilot wishes to achieve the best gliding angle over the ground in the presence of a head- or tailwind. Here, the situation corresponds to points M and N on

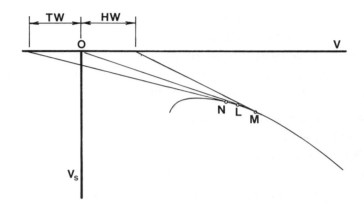

Fig. 12.7. Best speed to fly in the presence of a headwind (HW) or tailwind (TW).

the performance curve, and the pilot should set the MacCready ring to more or less than zero, depending on whether there is a head- or tailwind component, and again obeys the readings. This again is an illustration of the general result of Chapter 11. Just how much more or less than zero is not something which can easily be determined in flight, so again the pilot must use a mechanical analogue computer or, more usually, an electronic device. Strictly, the above construction is not quite correct, since in the presence of an up- or down-draught, the setting of the MacCready ring should be slightly varied, but in practice the above arrangement will suffice.

Use of Lee Waves

It is implicit in all of the above theories that the wind has no effect on the optimum speed for gliding between thermals, since both the climbs and glides are taking place in an air mass moving bodily over the countryside. Of course, as we have seen, the wind affects the break-off height from the last thermal, but the speed for the final glide is still that displayed by the MacCready ring.

Now, whereas thermals are assumed to move with the wind, some sources of lift remain more or less stationary with respect to the ground. In lee waves or simple hill lift, the pattern of streamlines in the atmosphere

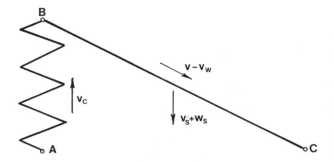

Fig. 12.8. Elementary cross-country using wave lift.

will remain stationary with the wind blowing through it. Imagine a cross-country flight conducted by climbing in a wave, gliding against the wind to the next wave, and so on. (See Fig. 12.8.) To a stationary observer, the diagram representing the flight looks like Fig. 8.2, except that the speed over the ground is $V - V_w$. The theory is then the same as for flying in thermals except that V is replaced by $V - V_w$ and hence the average speed is as in Eq. (8.8) with this substitution made. The average speed is then:

$$V_{av} = (V - V_w)V_c / (V_s + V_c + w_s) \qquad (12.6)$$

and the construction giving the speed to fly which maximises V_{av} is that of Fig. 12.9.

It is clear that if the MacCready ring is set to V_c, it will display an optimum speed V_2, which is too low. The correct speed is V_1, corresponding to a scaled-up ring setting V_c'. Assuming that the pilot has reasonable estimates of V_c and V_w he wishes to know the appropriate ring setting. Unfortunately, there is no simple solution to the problem which can be applied to simple instrumentation, although one could doubtless devise a computer which would display the correct speed to fly, having been fed with the correct values of V_w and V_c. Alternatively, if the pilot sets the MacCready ring to V_c and observes V_2, can he then derive the correct speed V_1 if he knows V_w? If one assumes the performance curve to be of the form of Eq. (4.12), then the calculation

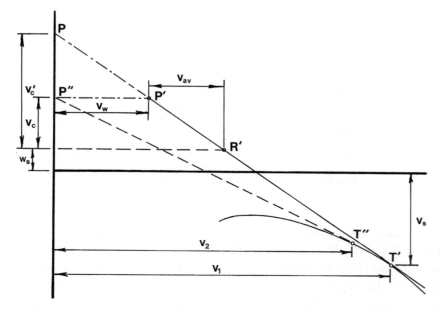

Fig. 12.9. Construction to give the best speed to fly for maximum average speed, using wave lift.

is quite straightforward, but is hardly something the pilot could produce off the top of his head whilst in flight. Also, it is unlikely that a computer would be produced to solve such a rarely-used calculation. Fortunately, a rough rule of thumb can be adduced, as follows:

(a) For low wind speeds (about one-quarter of the speed for best gliding angle), increase V_2 by half the wind speed.
(b) For high wind speeds (about the same as the speed for best gliding angle), increase V_2 by three-quarters of the wind speed.

References

The theory of this chapter has been taken from:

Welch, A. & L. and Irving, F. G., *New Soaring Flight,* John Murray, 1977 (with appropriate amendments to take into account the passage of time).

Chapter 13

THE EFFECT OF CENTRE
OF GRAVITY POSITION

It is common knowledge among soaring pilots that the tail lift force produces some extra induced drag, since the tail is simply a small wing. It is also common to suppose that down-loads are more unfavourable than up-loads, on the argument that up-loads relieve the wing lift, whilst down-loads increase it. On this basis, pilots have tended to think in terms of reducing the down-load on the tail at high speeds by ballasting the sailplane to get the centre of gravity (or centre of mass, as is now the more popular expression) at the aft limit (or perhaps even further aft). In fact a consequence of the mutual interference between the wing and tail is that the direction of the tail lift force is of no consequence. Other things being equal, a certain up-load on the tail produces the same increment in induced drag as a down-load of the same amount.

Long ago, Prandtl and Tietjens (1934) considered the total induced drag of biplanes, and this was enlarged upon by R.T. Jones in his excellent article in "Soaring" (1979), where he explains in some detail Munk's analysis of the total induced drag of a pair of lifting surfaces in tandem, such as a wing and tail, taking into account their mutual interference. It turns out that if the tail is producing a lift force, then for the same total lift, the induced drag is always greater than with zero tail lift and, moreover, the direction of the tail lift is of no consequence. Also, the relative fore- and aft-location of the surfaces is of no consequence: the result for a canard aircraft is the same as for a conventional layout. These results assume that the trailing vortex systems of the two surfaces are close to the same horizontal plane: with a T-tail, all of the results quoted here need some slight modification.

A consequence of this result is that an upward lift force is just as undesirable as a downward force. For a typical fixed geometry sailplane, whose CG position cannot be altered in flight, it would typically have a small up-load on the tail in slow circling flight and an appreciable down-load in fast straight flight, both of which will produce an increment in induced drag. Percentage-wise, the increment may well be greater at the higher speed but, since the induced drag is then a smaller proportion of the total drag, the actual drag increment in pounds could well be smaller than at low speeds. What interests the pilot is the loss of energy height due to the induced drag increments since this is, in effect, the extra height he has to gain in the course of a flight.

From Jones' paper, the total induced drag of the wing and tail of an aircraft, assuming that the vortex wakes of the two surfaces are close to the same horizontal plane, is

$$D_{1+2} = \left\{ W^2 / \pi q b_1^2 \right\} \left\{ 1 + \left[(b_1/b_2)^2 - 1 \right] \left[L_2/W \right]^2 \right\}. \qquad (13.1)$$

Since $W_2 / \pi q b_1^2$ represents the induced drag when $L_2 = 0$, the increment in induced drag due to the tail load is obtained by subtracting this quantity from the above expression, leaving

$$\Delta D_i = \left[L_2^2 / \pi q b_1^2 \right] \left[(b_1/b_2)^2 - 1 \right]. \qquad (13.2)$$

It should be noted that if the total lift is nW in circling flight, this equation will still apply if the effect of the vortex wakes becoming helical is neglected. L_2 must, of course, have the value appropriate to circling flight. Also, as noted above, the effect of the L_2^2 term is that the sign of L_2 is of no consequence.

If the sailplane flies for time t at speed V, then the loss of energy height due to the additional drag will be

$$\Delta h_e = \Delta D_i V t / W , \qquad (13.3)$$

it being assumed that the flight takes place near sea level. The conclusions on optimum CG position will be unaffected by the mean altitude.

Equation (13.2) may be re-written in terms of the maximum lift/drag ratio, the speed at which it occurs and the actual speed. Then if the proportion of time spent in circling flight is P_c it is possible to estimate the loss of energy height per hour. P_c is conveniently obtained by assuming that the classical theory applies, whence

$$P_c = \left[(V_g/V_o)^4 + 1 \right] / \left[3 (V_g/V_o)^4 - 1 \right] \qquad (13.4)$$

where V_g and V_o refer respectively to the gliding speed and the speed for maximum lift/drag.

The tail lift in circling flight is then given by

$$L_{2c} = \left[C_{mo} q_c Sc + (h - h_o) cnW \right] / l_i' \qquad (13.5)$$

where c is now the wing mean aerodynamic chord and n is the load factor whilst circling. Similarly, in gliding flight, q_c is replaced by q_g and now $n = 1$.

It is now a fairly straightforward process, for a sailplane of given characteristics, to select a certain dimensionless centre of gravity position, a likely circling speed and load factor, a likely gliding speed and to find P_c. This enables us to find the energy loss per hour due to circling flight and to straight flight and hence the total. This can be repeated for different values of h, so that the loss of energy height per hour can be plotted against h. The whole process can then be repeated for a new value of V_g.

Such calculations have been made for a typical Standard Class sailplane. It was assumed that the circling speed in thermals was 47 knots, and the angle of bank was 30°, thus giving a load factor of 1.22. For a gliding speed of 80 knots, the results were as follows:

Table 13.1

CG Position, h	Circling	$\Delta h_e/hr$, Gliding	Total
0.25	11.08	170.40	181.42
0.30	0.23	119.69	119.92
0.35	5.48	77.90	83.38
0.40	26.73	45.07	71.80
0.45	64.03	21.16	85.18
0.50	117.33	6.17	123.49

It will be seen that, with the CG well forward, the energy loss in the straight glide is predominant whilst when it is far aft, the energy loss in circling flight is the greater component. The overall loss is least when $b = 0.4$. At lower gliding speeds, the CG position for the least loss of total energy per hour comes forward, and is about 0.33 for a gliding speed of 60 knots. There does not seem to be any point in getting the CG aft of 0.40 × mean chord in this case, and 0.37 would be a good compromise: the energy loss per hour would be within a few feet of the optimum for any likely conditions.

When the sailplane has flaps, the calculations become a little more complicated, because C_{mo} has different values in the two conditions of flight. Some calculations for a 15-metre sailplane lead one to conclude that the effect of the flaps is to reduce the tail loads during the glide and hence the overall energy loss. Indeed, with the CG at 0.4 × mean chord and a glide speed of 60 knots, the total energy loss is quite negligible, since in this case the tail loads in both conditions of flight are very small. For this machine, the optimum CG position moves forward as the glide speed increases, due to the differing flap deflections at the various gliding speeds. Once again, the optimum CG position is about 0.4 × mean chord but if it were fixed at 0.37, the departure from optimum would be negligible.

These remarks do not apply to enormous Open Class sailplanes but, without doing the sums in detail, one suspects that the results would not be too different from those above. The important conclusion from the above is that there is no point in flying with an excessively aft CG position.

If, in the case of the Standard Class machine, the CG was movable, then the energy loss could be made zero in both conditions of flight. The time saved would then be about 7 secs per hour, or 0.02%, with a cruising speed of 70 knots. To shift the CG by the desired amount would involve moving a mass of about 18 lb through a distance of about 16 feet, doubtless by pumping water ballast. The aftmost CG position would be at 0.5 × mean chord, when the machine would be slightly unstable. To restore the stability, a slightly larger tailplane would be required, thus increasing the profile drag. Moving the CG in flight appears to be a profitless occupation.

Rough calculations for a T-tail sailplane suggest that the additional drag in circling flight is likely to be more, and in straight flight less, than that from the above calculations. The optimum CG is therefore likely to be further forward that suggested above. The results of C.O. Vernon (1992) tend to confirm these results.

References

Irving, F.G., "The optimum centre of gravity position for minimum overall energy loss", *OSTIV Publication* **XVI**, 1981.

Jones, R.T., "Minimising induced drag", *Soaring*, October, 1979.

Prandtl, L. and Tietjens, O.G., *Applied Hydro- and Aeromechanics*, Dover Publications, 1934 and 1957.

Vernon, C.O., "Trim drag", *Technical Soaring*, January, 1992.

Chapter 14

A BRIEF NOTE ON COMPUTERS, FLIGHT DATA RECORDERS, GPS, ETC.

Since *New Soaring Pilot* was written, it has become possible to obtain electronic devices which will perform most of the calculations required in soaring flight. Many of the more complex sums, previously impossible to carry out in the heat of the moment, are now little more than pressing a few buttons. The complexity of the devices varies enormously. On the one hand, a relatively simple contrivance will work like a normal audio variometer in thermals while also giving the rate of climb averaged roughly over the previous turn, becoming a-best-speed-to-fly indicator between thermals and storing a vast number of polars probably in a simplified form such as Eq. (3.2), with the capability to deal with various weights due to the presence or abscence of water ballast and because the appropriate chips are very cheap, a few extras such as temperature and battery volts are thrown in for good measure. At the other end of the scale is the device with built-in Global Positioning System (GPS), which not only carries out most of the calculations in this book but records the entire flight as well. It will also provide instantaneous data on a vast number of parameters. The price of such a device would have bought quite a sophisticated sailplane not many years ago and it comes with an instruction manual of amazing complexity.

At this point, I will refrain from enlarging on the difficulty of comprehending such manuals (at any rate to the older generation) and simply point out that some are more user-friendly than others. Indeed, the requirements for such an instrument can be summarized as follows:

It should be user-friendly, both in terms of the manual and the display;

It should deal in true airspeeds for all navigational purposes;

It should deal in equivalent airspeeds for all other purposes;

It should not display marginally useful data simply because it is simple to do so.

There is no doubt that the coming of the 'glass' cockpit represents a great step forward and some manufacturers are showing signs of making them simpler and friendlier.

Appendix 1

SOME USEFUL GENERAL REFERENCES

This book contains many references to OSTIV publications. OSTIV is the Organisation Scientifique et Technique Internationale de Vol a Voile and its address is: c/o TU-Delft, Fac. Aerospace Engin., Khuyverweg 1, NL-2629, HS Delft, The Netherlands. With a few exceptions, copies of the OSTIV references can be obtained from them. Why not become an Individual Member?

The Congress in Rieti, Italy, was the last for which an OSTIV Publication containing the proceedings was published. Thereafter, the proceedings were reproduced in "Technical Soaring", a joint publication of OSTIV and the Soaring Society of America. It is published quarterly by The Soaring Society of America, Inc., P.O. Box E, Hobbs, New Mexico 88241, USA.

Other general references are as follows:

1. Airworthiness.
1.1 "OSTIV Airworthiness Standards for Sailplanes", 1996.
1.2 "Joint Airworthiness Requirements: JAR 22, Sailplanes and Powered Sailplanes", Airworthiness Authorities Steering Committee, 1980, with subsequent changes. Obtainable from the Civil Aviation Authority, Printing and Publication Services, Greville House, 37, Gratton Road, Cheltenham, Glos., GL50 2BN, UK.

2. General.
2.1 Barnard, R.H. and Philpott, D.R., *Aircraft Flight*, Longman, 1989. (Concerned with powered aircraft but gives good general explanations.)
2.2 Brinkman, G. and Zacher, H., *Die Evolution der Segelflugzeuge*,

Bernard & Graefe Verlag, Heilsbachstrasse 26, D-5300 Bonn 1, Germany.

2.3 Coates, A., *Janes World Sailplanes and Motor Gliders*, Janes Publishing Co., 1980.

2.4 Reichmann, H., *Cross-Country Soaring*, Thomson Publications, 1978.

2.5 Stinton, D., *The Design of the Aeroplane*, Granada, 1983. (Mainly concerned with the aerodynamic design of light aeroplanes but contains much useful information.)

2.6 Torenbeek, E., *Synthesis of Subsonic Aeroplane Design,* Delft University Press/Martinus Nijhoff, 1982. (Mainly concerned with medium-sized transport aircraft, but contains much useful information.)

2.7 Welch, A. & L. and Irving, F.G., *The New Soaring Pilot*, John Murray, 1977. (Also published in the USA under the title *The Complete Soaring Pilot's Handbook* by David McKay Co. Inc., New York.)

3.   Aerodynamics.

3.1 Abbott, I.H. and von Doenhoff, A.E., *Theory of Wing Sections*, Dover, New York, 1958.

3.2 Althaus, D., *Stuttgarter Profilkatalog I*, Institut fur Aero- und Gasdynamik der Universitat Stuttgart, 1972.

3.3 Anderson, J.D., *Fundamentals of Aerodynamics*, McGraw-Hill, 1991.

3.4 Eppler, R., *Aerofoil Design and Data*, Springer-Verlag, 1990.

3.5 Hoerner, S.F., *Fluid Dynamic Drag*, Published by the author, 1965.

3.6 Kuethe, A.M. and Chow, C-Y., *Foundations of Aerodynamics*, John Wiley, 1986.

3.7 Simons, M., *Model Aircraft Aerodynamics*, Model and Allied Publications (Argus Books Ltd.), 1978. (Relates to models, but much of the material is also applicable to gliders.)

4.   Stability and Control.

4.1 Babister, A.W., *Aircraft Dynamic Stability and Response*, Pergamon, 1980.

4.2 Etkin, B., *Dynamics of Flight — Stability and Control*, 2nd Ed., John Wiley, 1982.

4.3 Irving, F.G., *An Introduction to the Longitudinal Static Stability of Low-Speed Aircraft*, Pergamon, 1966.

4.4 Morelli, P., "Static stability and control of sailplanes", *OSTIV*, 1976.

5.   Structures.

5.1 Kensche, Ch., "Fatigue of composite materials in sailplanes and rotor blades", *OSTIV Publication* **XVIII**, 1985.

5.2 Megson, T.H.G., *Aircraft Structures for Engineering Students*, Edward Arnold, 1977.

5.3 Roark, R.J., *Formulas for Stress and Strain*, McGraw-Hill, 1965.

5.4 Stender, W., "Sailplane weight estimation", *OSTIV*, 1969.

Appendix 2

CONVERSION FACTORS

Lengths, areas, volumes.

1 in = 2.54 cm, exactly	1 cm = 0.3937 in
1 ft = 0.3048 m	1 m = 3.2808 ft
1 statute mile = 5280 ft = 1.6093 km	1 km = 3281 ft = 0.6214 mile

1 nautical mile = 6080 ft
  = 1.515 statute miles = 1.8531 km

$1\ in^2 = 6.4516\ cm^2$	$1\ cm^2 = 0.1550\ in^2$
$1\ ft^2 = 0.0929\ m^2$	$1\ m^2 = 10.7639\ ft^2$

1 Imperial gallon = 1.2009 US gallon
  = 4.5455 litres

Masses and forces.

1 lb = 0.4536 kg	1 kg = 2.2046 lb
1 lbf = 4.4482 N	1 N = 0.2248 lbf
	1 daN = 1.0197 kp

Force per unit area.

$1\ lb/ft^2 = 4.8825\ kg/m^2$	$1\ kg/m^2 = 0.2048\ lb/ft^2$
$1\ lbf/in^2 = 0.0703\ kp/cm^2$	$1\ kp/cm^2 = 14.2248\ lbf/in^2$
$1\ bar = 10^5\ N/m^2$	$1\ millibar = 100\ N/m^2$

Miscellaneous.

Standard gravitational acceleration = $32.1740\ ft/sec^2$
  = $9.8066\ m/sec^2$
1 radian = 57.29°

Appendix 3

THE STANDARD ATMOSPHERE

Height	Temperature	Speed of sound	Pressure	Density, ρ	$(\rho/\rho_0)^{\frac{1}{2}}$
ft	°C	ft/sec	lb/ft^2	slug/ft^3	
0	15	1117	2116.2	0.002377	1.0000
1000	13.02	1113	2040.9	0.002308	0.9854
2000	11.04	1109	1967.7	0.002241	0.9710
3000	9.06	1105	1896.6	0.002175	0.9566
4000	7.08	1101	1827.7	0.002111	0.9424
5000	5.10	1098	1760.8	0.002048	0.9283
6000	3.11	1094	1695.9	0.001987	0.9143
7000	1.13	1090	1632.9	0.001927	0.9004
8000	−0.85	1086	1571.9	0.001868	0.8866
9000	−2.83	1082	1512.7	0.001811	0.8729
10 000	−4.81	1078	1455.3	0.001755	0.8594
11 000	−6.79	1074	1399.7	0.001701	0.8459
12 000	−8.77	1070	1345.9	0.001648	0.8326
13 000	−10.76	1066	1293.7	0.001596	0.8193
14 000	−12.74	1062	1243.2	0.001545	0.8062
15 000	−14.72	1058	1194.3	0.001496	0.7932
16 000	−16.70	1054	1146.9	0.001447	0.7804
17 000	−18.68	1050	1101.1	0.001401	0.7676
18 000	−20.66	1046	1056.8	0.001355	0.7549
19 000	−22.64	1041	1013.9	0.001310	0.7424
20 000	−24.62	1037	972.5	0.001266	0.7299

(cont'd)

Height	Temperature	Speed of sound	Pressure	Density, ρ	$(\rho/\rho_0)^{\frac{1}{2}}$
ft	°C	ft/sec	lb/ft^2	slug/ft^3	
25 000	−34.53	1016	785.3	0.001065	0.6694
30 000	−44.44	995	628.4	0.000889	0.6116
35 000	−54.34	973	498.0	0.000737	0.5567
36 089	−56.50	968	472.7	0.000706	0.5450
40 000	−56.50	968	381.7	0.000585	0.4962
50 000	−56.5	968	242.2	0.000362	0.3902
60 000	−56.5	968	149.8	0.000224	0.3068

SYMBOLS

A	Point on polar curve corresponding to minimum sink (Fig. 3.1)
A	Aspect ratio
A	Constant in Eq. (3.2)
a	Constant in Eq. (7.3)
a	Speed of sound
a_o	Two-dimensional lift curve slope
B	Point on polar curve corresponding to best gliding angle
B	Constant in Eq. (3.2)
b	Span
b	Constant in Eq. (7.3)
b_1	Wing span (In Eq. (13.1))
b_2	Tail span (In Eq. (13.1))
C_D	Drag coefficient
C_{Di}	Induced drag coefficient
C_{Do}	Profile drag coefficient, or minimum drag coefficient
C_L	Lift coefficient
C_{Mo}	Pitching moment coefficient about the aerodynamic centre
C_p	Pressure coefficient, $p/\frac{1}{2}\rho V^2$
c	Constant in Eq. (7.3)
D	Drag
ΔD	Increment in drag

g	Acceleration due to gravity
g_o	Acceleration due to gravity at $Z = 0$
h	Height
h	Dimensionless CG position aft of mean aerodynamic centre
h_A	Height required to cover a given distance at maximum L/D
h_e	Energy height
H_e	Change of energy height between x_1 and x_2
k	Induced drag factor
L	Lift
L_2	Tail lift
l	Length
l_1'	Distance between the aerodynamic centre of tail and aerodynamic centre of the rest of the glider
m	Mass of sailplane
n	Load factor, L/W
n	An index, as in ρ^n
p_s	Static pressure of the atmosphere
P_c	Proportion of time spent in circling flight
q	Angular velocity about Oy or the centre of curvature of the flight path
q	Dynamic head per unit area, $\frac{1}{2}\rho V^2$
q_c	Dynamic head per unit area in circling flight
q_g	Dynamic head per unit area in gliding flight
R	Radius of turn
R	Thermal radius (i.e., the value of r at which $V_T = 0$)
R_e	Reynolds number
r	Angular velocity about Oz

r	Radius in a thermal
S	Gross wing area
T	Thrust
T	Time constant of variometer
T	Time to travel from x_1 to x_2
t	Time
t_c	Climbing time
t_g	Gliding time
V	True airspeed
V_{av}	Average speed for a cross-country flight
V_c	True rate of climb
V_D	Design diving speed
V_{DF}	Demonstrated diving speed
V_g	Gliding speed
V_i	Equivalent airspeed
V_{ims}	Equivalent airspeed for minimum rate of sink
V_{io}	Equivalent airspeed for best L/D
V_{ne}	Never-exceed speed
V_{opt}	Optimum gliding speed for max overall speed
V_s	True rate of sink
V_{si}	Equivalent rate of sink
$V_{si\,min}$	Eqivalent minimum rate of sink
$V_{s\,ind}$	Indicated rate of sink
V_{sio}	Eqivalent rate of sink at best L/D
V_w	Headwind component
V_{weff}	Effective headwind
V_T	Strength of thermal at radius r
V_{To}	Strength of thermal at $r = 0$
V_{tr}	Velocity along the track
V_1	Speed for minimum sink at $n = 1$
V_ϕ	Speed for minimum sink at an angle of bank ϕ

V_{s1}	Minimum sinking speed for $n = 1$
$V_{s\phi}$	Minimum sinking speed at an angle of bank ϕ
v	True airspeed (Kantrowitz's letter, Chapter 5)
W	Weight of the sailplane
w	Wing loading, W/S
w	Upwards air velocity (Chapter 10)
w_s	Rate of sink of air
w^*	$1/\lambda$
X	Distance to go along the flight path
x	Generalised distance along the flight path
Z	Geopotential altitude

Greek Symbols

α	Angle of incidence (or attack)
ε	Downwash angle
ε	Angle between the thrust and the Ox axis
Φ	Angle of roll about Ox
ϕ	Angle of bank whilst circling
Γ	Slope of flight path
λ	Lagrange multiplier
λ	Angle between course and track
μ	Viscosity
Ω	Angular velocity about a vertical axis
ρ	Air density
ρ_o	Standard sea-level air density
θ	Angle between Ox and the horizontal

INDEX

LIST OF AUTHORS QUOTED
AT THE END OF EACH CHAPTER